A Bridge to
LANDSCAPE
QUILTS

Mary L. Hackett

American Quilter's Society

P. O. Box 3290 • Paducah, KY 42002-3290

www.AmericanQuilter.com

Located in Paducah, Kentucky, the American Quilter's Society (AQS) is dedicated to promoting the accomplishments of today's quilters. Through its publications and events, AQS strives to honor today's quiltmakers and their work and to inspire future creativity and innovation in quiltmaking.

EDITOR: TRACEY JOHNSON
GRAPHIC DESIGN: AMY CHASE
COVER DESIGN: MICHAEL BUCKINGHAM
QUILT PHOTOS: CHARLES R. LYNCH
SCENIC PHOTOS: MARY L. HACKETT

Library of Congress Cataloging-in-Publication Data

Hackett, Mary L.
    A bridge to landscape quilts / by Mary L. Hackett.
        p. cm.
    ISBN 1-57432-856-5
    1. Patchwork--Patterns. 2. Appliqué. 3. Quilting. 4. Fabric pictures. 5. Landscape in art. I. Title

    TT835.H23 2004
    746.46'041--dc22

                    2004015073

Additional copies of this book may be ordered from the American Quilter's Society, PO Box 3290, Paducah, KY 42002-3290, or online at www.americanquilter.com.

Dedicated to

Mary Ellen Kinder, the first quilter in my life;

Frances Bahr, my godmother and beloved aunt;

and Lela Kinder Bahr—who never really let me go.

Contents

Walking Panda

Faith is the substance of things hoped for, the evidence of things not seen.

—The Holy Bible, Hebrews 11:1

For a number of years, my husband's work required him to rise at 5 a.m. When we married, I was a night owl who enjoyed working till 1 a.m. and sleeping as long as humanly possible. However, I chose to get up with Walt so that we could enjoy breakfast together before he left for work, and thus began my new, more intimate relationship with nature. Walt and I are blessed to live in a wooded location where the light first comes through a stand of oaks, hickories, sycamores, pines, and dogwoods before it reaches our windows. So we actually woke up each morning in the dark, or close to it.

Between the time Walt left for his commute and my work started, I began to discover a lovely play of light outside our windows. One day, a blush of pink came through the trees and I hurried to dress for walking our Australian shepherd, Panda. But the light was quickly changing, and I missed the show! Some mornings, I ran around the backyard in my robe and slippers, taking pictures of morning glow, shadows falling across glistening grass, shafts of light through naked trees, and other simple wonders of a sunrise in the woods.

Walks with Panda took us across an open meadow toward the local community college, where I took pictures of a lone oak tree standing in the middle of the field, and a close-up of frost clinging to grass and leaves. Near the creek that feeds a small man-made lake, trees crowded the edge of the water, casting reflections on its surface. Sometimes a great blue heron took wing as I approached, or ducks landed near the fountain. No matter the time of year or the time of day, I always found that path enchanting.

This woman is easily entertained, you may be thinking. Perhaps, but I think an appreciation of the outdoors (or of any visual stimulation, for that matter) lies in our sensitivity to and actual observation of our surroundings. To adapt to a complex world, we have learned to suppress much of that visual sensitivity.

To produce landscape designs in fabric that will bring you pleasure and satisfaction, you first need to be able to determine what you like. My aim is to help you notice how you perceive what you see, which images you favor, and how to interpret them in fabric. It's like figuring out a puzzle, putting components together, and coming up with your own personal solution. It's amazing and it's fun!

My husband, Walt, with Panda and Weegie

Bridging the Gap

Introduction

I love patchwork, don't you? I love the way it looks. I love its scrappy history. I love the way it goes together. Whether I'm working by hand or by machine, one of my favorite things in the world is to sit and sew together strings of colorful patches.

At the machine, I merrily chain piece squares or assembly-line sew Log Cabin blocks. In front of the television, I hand piece set-in blocks or endless lines of triangles, while my husband dutifully fills me in on the action I have missed ... the action that most interests me is taking shape in my lap!

So, as my desire to make landscapes as fabric paintings has evolved, I still use some traditional techniques in every quilt. Though the illusion of reality is my main goal, I want very much to maintain a landscape's connection to its origin; that is, to celebrate my work's "quiltness." Patchwork allows me to do that. Even those landscapes that appear more like a painting from a distance give up their secrets on close inspection.

For the vast majority of quilters, we are discussing a recreational activity, a hobby, a means to make beautiful, useful things to pass on to family members and treasured friends. There are no hard-and-fast rules for applying any of my suggestions ... just guidelines that reflect my experiences in sewing and what has worked for me. My hope is that you will understand the concepts, enjoy the process at your own pace, and learn to make results that please you. Lovely quilted landscapes can be made using everyday sewing techniques only ... this is "The Bridge to Landscape Quilts"

The Bridge
Follow a Familiar Path

Photo 1. GARDEN BRIDGE IN SPRING, 27" X 39½", by the author. The bridge pictured in this quilt is in my backyard garden. (Pattern begins on page 60.)

The bridge to landscape quilts ...

You can make landscape quilts with the sewing skills and materials that are already familiar to most quilters. No particular talent, techniques, fabrics, or tools are necessary for you to begin.

is built of traditional techniques.

To make landscape quilts, we will combine the various techniques in a building-block manner, matching the technique to the natural objects in our fabric picture. Then we will think about the fabric choices on a patch-by-patch basis.

New Ways to Use Traditional Techniques

Traditional pieced blocks will become the large areas of your landscape design. Sky, water, and land sections can be made of pieced blocks, letting the wonderful geometric shapes lend a subtle texture to these areas. Choosing the fabric for each patch within the block is like choosing a dab of paint from your artist's palette. Change a patch and you change the look.

Patchwork

My favorite technique for relaxation, creative satisfaction, and just plain versatility is hand piecing. Because so few blocks are needed for a landscape quilt, no pattern is too difficult. With the flexibility of hand piecing, you can set in patches, make intricate patterns, and even work while on the road or watching television.

The secret bonus is that this bit of patchwork will be only part of a lovely landscape and thus partially covered or cut up (ouch!) to insert other components. As a result, errors (who, me?) in piecing, pressing, or matching points, will be totally obscured by the other wonderful sewing techniques of the piece. See? I told you this would be fun!

Machine Techniques

If you prefer, machine piecing is just dandy, too. While at the machine, you may want to try straight strip piecing, crazy quilting, paper piecing, and Celtic bias strips. Strip piecing is simply the sewing together of strips of fabric of any width. The seam allowances can be pressed to one side or open, and the resulting yardage can be cut up and used in any way you like. Strip piecing works well for sunset skies, land rolling away into the distance, or sunbeams coming through the trees.

Photo 2. DREAM LOVER, 122" x 85", by the author. This aerial view of the landscape is strip-pieced and the flying figure is appliquéd.

Any section of your landscape may be sewn, in crazy-quilt fashion, on a muslin or paper foundation. Paper piecing may be used for a more precise rendition of a particular section of your landscape. These techniques can be used to mimic foliage and flowers, rough rocks, or white water.

Appliqué

For making trees, fence posts, and other narrow objects, try Celtic bias strips, bias tape, or folded straight strips. All appliqué techniques, either hand or machine, can be employed for specific features. That includes my personal favorite, freezer-paper appliqué.

Any shape you can imagine, you can add to your landscape when appliqué is in your bag of tricks. The full moon, buildings, foliage, water, animals—the list is endless.

If you find your quilting skills lacking in any technique, I suggest that you check out a good book on the subject or tap your local resources for a little hands-on instruction. So much good information is available on traditional quilting techniques that I will not be addressing the specific how-tos, but there will be a few tips that have worked for me thrown in from time to time.

You have the quilting skills. The rest is simply the willful act of allowing your mind to let go of what you think you can or can't do. It entails getting past what is "right" when it comes to quilting, of training yourself to really see the natural things around you, and employing well-loved quilting techniques to simulate them.

Let's give it a try!

Preparing the Fabric Paint Box

In making a landscape quilt, you can put your stash to good use. To get in the mood, let's discuss the kinds of fabrics that can be successful in a landscape. You may be surprised.

Photo 3. ONCE AND FUTURE HOME (detail), by the author. The fabrics used to create the leaves, stones, and grass do not mimic the actual elements of nature but give the appearance of those elements seen from a distance.

First and foremost, I think it's a good idea to *start with your comfort level*. We may stretch that comfort level in the process, but you will most likely enjoy working with your favorite colors and your favorite prints. Believe it or not, many of the fabrics intended for a traditional block quilt will work well if used judiciously in a landscape composition.

The value of a fabric (light to dark) is much more important than the actual figurative design of its print. For example, see figure 1–1 for a comparison of solids to prints that read as solids. Notice how the print, whatever its subject matter, adds a degree of texture that is absent in the solid. Figure 1–2 shows a variety of monochromatic prints useful in landscapes. A flow of color or value across a fabric makes it a good candidate for our purposes.

 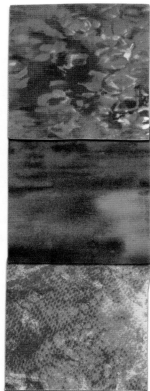

Fig. 1–2. Values within prints

Fig. 1–1. Textured solids

Figure 1–3 is a selection of repeat prints. A uniform, identifiable pattern can be obvious if the patch used will be large enough for the repeat to appear several times. For a small patch, a tiny print can be just right, with its repeat providing texture and color, rather than being a distraction. Therefore, the larger a fabric

Fig. 1–3. Repeat patterns

piece will be, the more important it is to notice and control how much pattern repeat will be apparent.

My personal pleasure in fabric selection is to use fabrics that approximate natural components when seen from a distance but that do not actually mimic them. I think this is a more interesting approach than searching out novelty prints representing sky, stones, trees, etc. In addition, you can avoid purchasing fabrics that you will never use for another purpose. I like using scraps of clothing with sentimental ties, unusual materials for their textural qualities, and unexpected add-ons. Examples of prints that can subtly contribute to your illusion are shown in figure 1–4.

Fig. 1–5. Novelty prints

Fig. 1–4. Better choices than novelty prints

Sometimes, however, nothing will do but a brick print, for example, and because it is available, why not? Figure 1–5 compares some prints that are usable and some that are more problematic. If you've already got'em, sew'em, but think border and backing for them rather than the scenery portion of your quilt.

Searching for Fabric

To choose a fabric for a particular area of your design, prioritize your search using these criteria:

- **Value.** This is even more important than color in choosing a fabric, so you may want to get into the habit of arranging your stash according to lights, mediums, and darks within each color family. Avoid overuse of mid-range values or your pictures may seem to melt together.

- **Color.** It may seem obvious to look for blues for your sky and water, but you will learn to expand from there. Prints with subtly mixed colors are wonderful.

- **Texture.** What "feel" is brought to mind by your fabric choice? Smooth, shiny, shaggy, rough? It matters.

- **Scale.** A print whose size is obviously out of line with its location in your scene will upset the illusion of reality.

- **Temperature.** Huh? Consider, have you noticed that yellow-green and blue-green evoke differing atmospheres? Have you noticed that lemon yellow is "cooler" than golden yellow?

- **Distractions.** No matter how much you like a fabric, if it seems to jump out of the picture, it can interrupt your whole composition!

- **You like it!** True love can trump any and all of the above considerations.

Quick Fixes

When you can't find a fabric that is perfect, consider these "fixes" for a candidate that is close but falls a little short:

- **Value.** Try using the reverse of the fabric to lighten the effect. If you want to go darker, try tea-dying a swatch. To make a print more sky-like or to mimic a sunrise, scrunch the fabric and dip a portion of it in a weak solution of bluing.

- **Color.** If you just love a series of fabrics that are unlike nature, let color become the theme of your landscape. For example, see LONE OAK, page 29, and BLUE MORNING, page 32.

- **Texture.** The right color in the wrong texture can add interest to the patchwork in your border.

- **Scale.** Try moving the out-of-scale fabric to a location that corresponds better with its size. If it doesn't seem to fit but you still love it, save it for use in the border.

- **Temperature.** If the majority of your fabric choices are either warm or cool, attempt to change out the minority to that temperature for a consistent mood. If you must mix temperatures to achieve the representational look you want, try to strike a balance. Be aware that sunlit areas are mostly warm and shadow areas are mostly cool.

- **No distractions.** Cut out problem areas or cover them with appliqué elements. A small print with light spots that "pop" can be touched up with a permanent pen, or the print can be tea-dyed or tan-dyed.

- **Hey, it's your quilt!** If you love the fabric, use it. Then choose other fabrics for your composition to complement it.

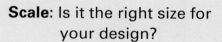

It's tempting, but ...

Using commercial novelty prints representing sky, stone, water, etc., brings up these questions:

Scale: Is it the right size for your design?

Value: Is it a mid-range value (most are) that detracts from your light-shade illusion?

Mood: Is it too cartoony?

Color: Does it really fit into your scheme?

Instead, use those prints in your border patchwork or on the back of your quilt.

The Verge

One of the most useful characteristics of some commercially produced fabrics is the place where colors or textures converge. This "verge" allows for a blurring effect, an edge that is difficult to achieve by appliqué or by piecing individual patches of fabric (fig. 1–6). If you find a fabric with a verge of useful colors (a variety of values within a color family or a movement from, say, yellow to red), buy it! The verge area can become a shadow on a tree trunk, a sunrise or sunset, the blush on a flower petal. I have bought fabric that I have no particular use for, except that is has verge areas, because of its contribution to the illusion. Delightful!

 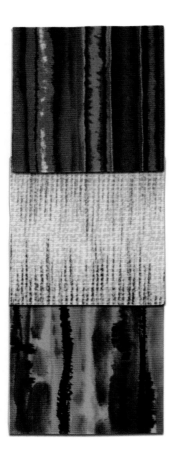

Fig. 1–6. The verge

Threads and Other Supplies

Threads and the materials you will need for batting and backing are the same as for other quilts you have made. The characteristics of certain non-traditional materials, however, also make them reasonable candidates for a small quilt intended for hanging on a wall. These things are discussed in Quilting Your Landscape on page 33, and the decisions can be put off until you have gained some experience with my seat-of-the-pants approach to all quilting issues.

Meantime, think playtime for grownups!

Seeing Is Believing

Picasso once said that art is a lie that tells us the truth. Hmmm. Much to consider there. In the most concrete sense, art is, in fact, a lie … that is, an illusion. It is not reality, but an interpretation of reality. When we make art, we are by definition expressing our innermost responses to the world. It is no more mysterious than that.

Understanding What You See

If you are like me, you want to create a scene that is beautiful, realistic enough to set a mood, and one that has no obvious errors to destroy the pleasant illusion. To interpret reality to a degree that makes it recognizable to ourselves and to others, we first must *see reality accurately.*

So let's think about the way we visually perceive things and how our brains identify what we see. This will not be a scientific analysis of optics and brain cells but an overview of the visual cues that help us place ourselves within our environment.

Betty Edwards, in her book *Drawing on the Right Side of the Brain*, calls this "expanding your perceptual powers." Stop reading now, and look around the room. Look at something close to you and then at something as far away as you can see, even out a window. How does your eye (and thus your brain) know that one thing is closer and the other is farther away? Look at figure 1–7, on page 14. Which tree is the largest? Which is the smallest? How do you know? In the process of answering this question, you will begin to sharpen your "skills in seeing."

• **Scale** is one clue. The size of something as it relates to you gives information about where it is located. A cup sitting near you, the television on the other side of the room, the chair in the corner … all are scaled to your body size, and if they are in the room with you, they are perceived as life-sized and thus close by. Your experience, on the other hand, tells you that if a tree looks small, if you can see all of it from the ground to its crown, it is a good distance from you. But what if there is a miniature tree in the

Fig. 1–7. Which tree is the largest?

room in which you sit? The scale of the things you can see around the tree will help here. The miniature tree will be on a table, perhaps. The life-sized tree will be somewhere outside, beyond the window. That, of course, brings us to perspective.

• **Perspective** is the visual effect of things appearing smaller in the distance. We learned in school that the road seems to disappear as it approaches the horizon, even though it is just as wide there as at our feet. Any linear feature, such as a road, fence, railroad, or line of trees, that appears to diminish in size gradually, indicates to our eye (and thus our brain) that we are looking into the distance. This effect may be observed in the room in which you are sitting (fig. 1–8, page 15). For example, if there are matching lamps and you are closer to one than the other, which one will be smaller? The lamps also cast light, which brings us to the source of light, another visual cue.

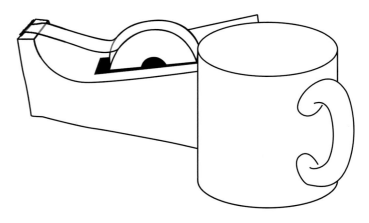

Fig. 1–9. Which object is closer to you? How do you know?

Fig. 1–8. Pictures on a wall. Which is closer? How do you know?

- **The source of light** helps us place ourselves in our surroundings and gives shape to what we see. Shadows, whether deep or subtle, give us cues about the location of an object, its size and shape, and its relationship to ourselves. You will notice this in the light that falls across the furniture in the room in which you sit. Now try to imagine that you are driving down a road, with the sun low in the sky to your right. You may see shadows cast across the road ahead of you. Pretend that, instead, the large truck ahead of you casts a shadow down the road toward you. This effect would confuse you, whether consciously or not, because you are experiencing light from the side, and for shadows to fall toward you, you would need to be driving into the sun.

- **Overlapping images** are strong visual cues indeed. One might imagine that this is a simple concept, but it is surprising how many compositional errors are made when placing images in a landscape or a still life. The fact is, two objects cannot occupy the same space. When you look at figure 1–9, you perceive the cup as sitting in front of the tape dispenser and closer to you. We cannot see through things, and so a house fully visible must be closer to us than one overlapped by its neighbor, regardless of their relative sizes.

- **Perceived detail** gives us a cue about the location of an object. We may be able to see every blade of grass at our feet and the petals of a flower a few feet away. However, portraying every leaf on every tree on the other side of the lake is not only a waste of time but will actually diminish the illusion of distance we are trying to establish.

Now look at (or imagine) a stand of trees (fig. 1–10, page 16) and try to determine exactly how you know that there is a group of trees, not a monolithic something that is all the same color. Value (the lightness or darkness of a color) will play a part as you observe the group of trees, as will scale, perspective, source of light, and overlapping images. Do you see any other aspects of this picture that we have not mentioned? How do you think they affect the way you relate yourself as the viewer to what you see? Try to become more aware, day by day, not only of what you see, but also how you perceive what you are seeing.

A Landscape in Progress

Let's put these ideas into play to understand their impact on the basic decisions you can make about a composition. Starting with a horizontal arrangement (fig. 1–11, page 16) of three trees, a slope, and the sun, what do you see?

Fig. 1–10. Your brain instantly analyzes visual cues as you walk down a woodsy path.

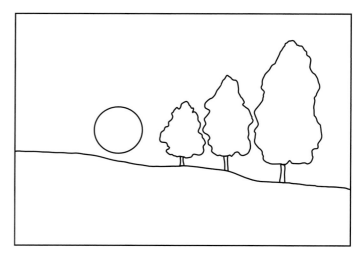

Fig. 1–11. This drawing has three trees, a slope, and a sun ... or does it?

Fig. 1–12. The scene looks flat and surreal.

The scene meets classic criteria you may already know, such as avoiding placing the horizon line or major components smack in the center. It has a variety of scale, one might think, and even an implication of perspective caused by the sizes of the trees. But wait ... how do you know where the trees are located in relationship to each other? To the viewer? What evidence do you have that the disk is the sun rather than, say, a hot air balloon?

With the scant information this composition provides, we know only that the trees increase in size the farther they are from the disk. Assuming that the circle is the sun, which would give off light, let's add shadows to the trees to help locate them in the composition (fig. 1–12). If the trees are all on the same plane, each is screened from the sun by the tree next to it, and the largest tree receives light only near the top. Somehow, this just doesn't look natural.

What if we assume that the increasing size *does* imply perspective, that is, that the largest tree is closest to us and the smallest the farthest away? In that case, each tree would receive more light from the sun (fig. 1–13, page 17). But are they lined up like bowling pins? What other cues do we have that any of the trees is actually closer to us? We begin to feel uncomfortable with this, as our senses "fight" with what we are seeing.

So let's move to *overlapping images* to remedy the flatness of this picture. Adding one or two lines below the horizon instantly suggests a rolling terrain, as in

Fig. 1–13. Changing the shadows should help define the location of the trees. Does it?

figure 1–14. Our mental response is to "see" distance as the land seems to fall away.

Pushing the disk down slightly behind the horizon makes it seem more like a setting sun, thus giving us "permission" to make the sky a gloriously colored patchwork. Let's rearrange the trees a little, so that they overlap the land areas and each other. As a final invitation for the viewer to enter the landscape, let's add a road or path that skirts the contour of the land.

With this new information, we can apply shadows accurately because we can imagine the light source,

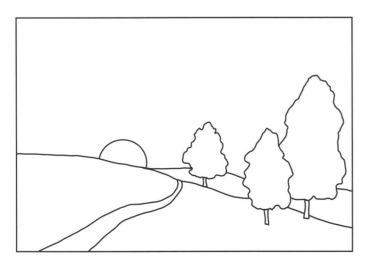

Fig. 1–14. Overlapping images and contours in the land contribute to a sense of realism.

predict how it would hit the trees, and add shadows cast on the slopes to further enhance the illusion of form. In the pencil sketch, we can even add color. The result is figure 1–15. So, what do you think?

Fig. 1–15. Accurate shadows round out our landscape: (a) black and white pencil sketch, (b) colored pencil sketch of the same landscape.

Other visual cues will enhance or diminish the accuracy of your fabric landscape and thus your ability to express your creative vision. We will discuss them in more detail as we begin to design and sew fabric landscapes. What you see is what you make, so learning to observe accurately will improve your sewing skills.

Now, wasn't that easy?

Nice and Easy

Your First Project

In spite of its lush look, this landscape project is really quite basic and easy to make. It will provide an opportunity for you to add your personal stamp to its simplicity and beauty so you can experience immediate success. It is a practice piece, so just relax and enjoy making it.

Making a Basic Landscape

This woodland scene is a simple composition (fig. 2–1). The design incorporates traditional block construction, strip piecing, a little appliqué, and slightly curved piecing. Options are offered for more complex and therefore more richly textured details.

Please read through the whole process before you begin to sew because we will be covering the visual cues mentioned in Seeing Is Believing, page 13. You will understand how they can make the difference between a somewhat primitive picture and one that crosses the "reality line" into Wow!

Sky Section A

1. Choose a wide variety of light blue fabrics to make four quilt blocks.

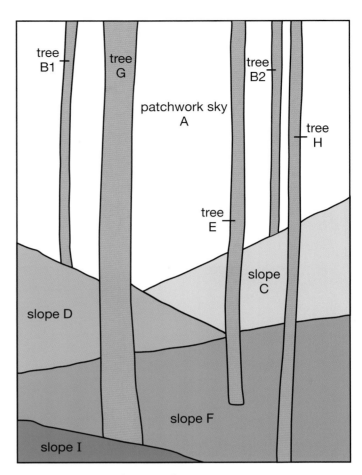

Fig. 2–1. Elements of your landscape

The size of the blocks will determine the size of your landscape. For example, I began with 8" traditional Windblown Star blocks from Judy Martin's *Scrap Quilts* (Leman Publications, 1985). Any block will do for our purposes, even four different blocks,

Fabric Requirements	Cotton Prints Recommended	
Landscape element	Colors	Amounts
Sky section A	Very light to light blues for four 8" blocks	Scraps
Trees B1, B2, E, G, H	Light to dark browns	Strips will do, 3"–4" x 20"–22"
Slopes C, D, F, I	Light to dark greens	Fat quarters or large scraps

Photo 4. (opposite page) THROUGH THE TREES, by the author. This quilt was inspired by early spring views of my backyard.

as long as they are the same size. The instructions given assume 8" blocks, so if you choose a pattern significantly larger or smaller, adjust the instructions accordingly.

Unlike blocks for a bed quilt, you will want to avoid rigid repetition of color in your sky block patches. Instead, to mimic a wonderful sky, choose a variety of light blues (fig. 2–2). Fabrics with flecks of other colors are great, but you won't want to include jarring prints or colors that are unnatural for a sky.

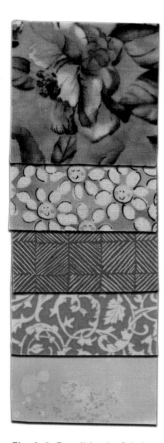

Fig. 2–2. Possible sky fabrics

Pull light blue scraps and arrange them from darkest to lightest, check the reverse side of the medium blues for a lighter version of the front side, and don't reject non-sky prints. You will be using only small amounts of each fabric, but each fabric's value and color are much more important than the print. Use as great a variety of scraps as you can.

2. Cut the patches for your blocks from the blue fabrics.

   You have probably noticed on a clear day that the sky seems lighter near the horizon and a deeper blue overhead. This effect will be achieved in your patchwork if you arrange the patches with lighter blues on the bottom and darker blues at the top. In addition, this bright sky is our light source, as discussed in Seeing Is Believing, page 13.

3. Lay out the patches for all four blocks at once and view them as a unit, arranging and rearranging the patches until you achieve a pleasing look.

   With low contrast, the pattern will create a gentle flow of color, rather than a bed quilt behind the trees. The interested viewer will discover your lovely blocks in the background. The casual viewer will see only a natural-looking sky.

   Just play with your scraps, auditioning them in different locations. Try squinting or lowering the room lighting until your eye sees a movement of color across the patchwork rather than a high contrast in any location.

4. Sew the patches into blocks and join the four blocks to make a square for sky section A (fig. 2–3).

Fig. 2–3. Sky section A

Distant Trees B1 and B2

1. Cut sky section A into three sections. (Yikes!)

Refer to figure 2–4. Notice that the cutting lines are gentle curves because real trees are not straight as posts. You can use a rotary cutter with no ruler to help you achieve a smooth curve. Just begin at the bottom of the fabric and slice toward the top of the sky. The exact location of these cuts is not crucial, but you will want to avoid coming within ½" of any bulky seams in the patchwork sky.

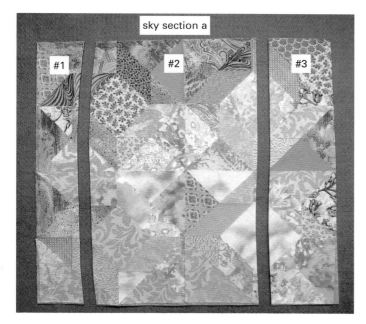

Fig. 2–4. Make gently curved cuts to divide the sky into three pieces.

You now have three pieces of sky patchwork. Number them 1–3, left to right. The cut edges will be your guides for cutting strips of fabric for the most distant trees.

2. Choose your tree fabrics.

To enhance a feeling of depth, make the most distant trees the lightest color, with the trees becoming gradually darker as they advance toward the viewer. The best choices for these two trees would be light to medium fabrics that read as solids.

3. Insert the first tree: Lay out the fabric you have chosen for tree B1, right side up. Place sky piece 1 (also right side up) on top of the tree fabric. Place sky piece 2 next to it, realigning the raw cut edges of the patchwork.

4. Move piece 2 slowly to the right, keeping the patchwork seams aligned as you open a gap revealing the tree fabric below. Adjust this gap until it is about ¾" wide. If you stand back, you can see what your tree will look like.

5. Use chalk or a sliver of soap to mark the tree fabric along the cut edges of sky pieces 1 and 2. Also draw a line at the top and bottom across the gap. This will aid in realignment of all pieces when you sew.

6. Remove the sky pieces and use a rotary cutter with no ruler to cut out tree B1, adding about ¼" seam allowance all around your marks.

7. Match tree B1 right sides together with the cut edge of sky piece 1, aligning your top and bottom marks with the top and bottom of the sky piece. Sew this gently curving seam with a scant ¼" seam allowance. Press the new seam allowance toward tree B1 (fig. 2–5).

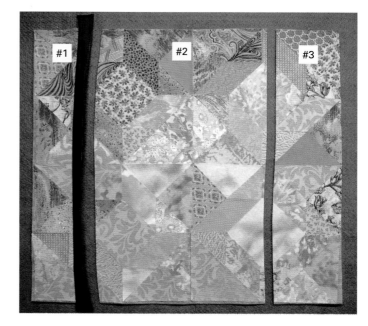

Fig. 2–5. Tree B1 sewn to sky piece 1.

8. Now lay sky piece 2 on top of tree B1, right sides together. Align any obvious seam lines in the sky patchwork so that the sky seems to continue unbroken behind the tree trunk. Sew as before, then press the seam allowances toward the tree.

Notice that tree B1 stands out slightly from the surface, which contributes to the illusion that it stands in front of your beautiful sky.

9. Just as you did with tree B1, cut and insert tree B2 (fig. 2–6).

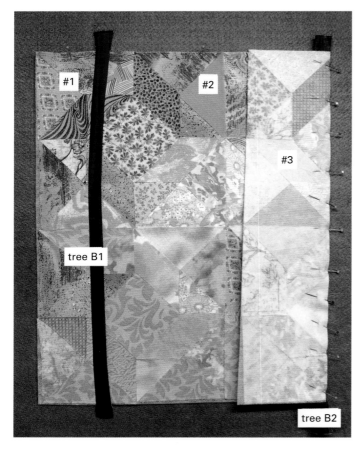

Fig. 2–6. Sew sky piece 3 to tree B2.

Note that your piece is now slightly wider than its beginning width of approximately 16" (fig. 2–7). It will grow again, almost a living thing in your hands!

Slope C

Add slope C with a straight or slightly curved seam that is angled across sky A and tree B2, as shown in figure 2–8.

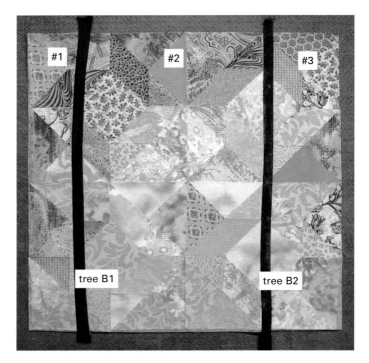

Fig. 2–7. Your sky and background trees are now complete.

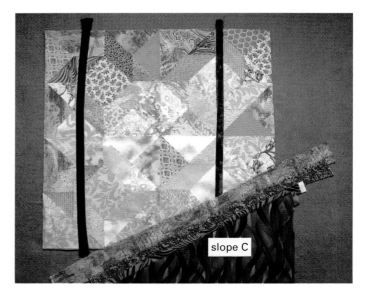

Fig. 2–8. Slope C is strip pieced from three fabrics.

Slope C should be the lightest one because the sunlight falls across it. You could use a single scrap of print fabric, or you could add to the texture of this and other slopes by strip piecing selected fabrics. These need to be lighter in the distance, becoming somewhat darker as they advance toward the viewer.

If you choose a patterned fabric for any of the slopes, make sure that its scale is in concert with the size of the trees on that slope.

Sky section A can be trimmed away under slope C, if you like, or left intact to help stabilize subsequent seams.

Appliqué Alternative

The inset method takes a fraction of the time and effort needed to appliqué the tree trunks in the traditional way. But if you want to cut strips and appliqué them to the background, go ahead. I promise I won't send out the Quilt Police!

Fig. 2–9. Cut for inserting tree E

Slope D and Tree E

1. For slope D, place a scrap of fabric across tree B1 and slope C. Sew slope D to the landscape.

   Slope D should be somewhat darker than slope C, or matched in value to the darkest strip in slope C.

   Be sure that the scrap is large enough to reach the left side of the quilt and that it extends past the insertion point for tree E on the right.

2. To add tree E, first cut the landscape apart as shown in figure 2–9, then cut the tree fabric as before. Tree E should be darker in value than trees B1 and B2 and, of course, somewhat wider.

3. Join both sides of the tree to the cut landscape sections, sewing from the top of the sky to just before you reach slope D. Leave the rest of the trunk unsewn so that slope F can be inserted under it (fig. 2–10).

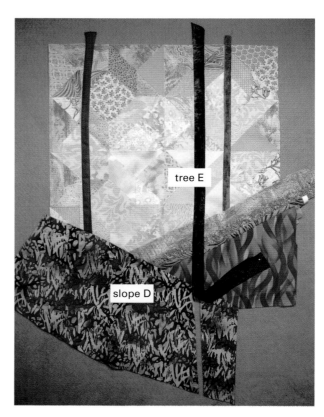

Fig. 2–10. Add tree E, but stop sewing before you reach slope D.

Gentle Slopes Without Appliqué

Curved slopes can be appliquéd, if you like, but here's another way to make gently curving slopes.

1. Place the slope fabric (right side up with the grain line aligned with the trees) on top of the landscape; pin in place. Decide where you would like the slope line (A). Draw a line on the fabric roughly ½" below the desired slope line. Be sure the line runs from the side edge of the landscape to below where the slope will be covered by the next slope. Add marks where the landscape piece and the slope fabric intersect to aid in matching the edges for sewing (B).

2. Cut on the drawn line through all layers of fabric. Discard the slope fabric above the cut. Discard the landscape fabric underneath the slope fabric (C).

3. Align the cut edge of the slope and the landscape piece, right sides together. Pin and sew this curve, easing the seam as you would any gentle curve (D).

4. Press the seam allowances toward the slope (E). As with the tree seam allowances, this contributes to the illusion that this slope is closer to the viewer than the previous trees and slopes.

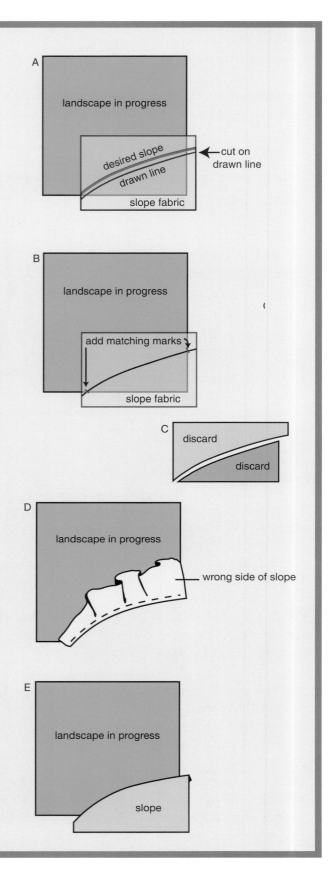

A
landscape in progress
desired slope
drawn line
cut on drawn line
slope fabric

B
landscape in progress
add matching marks
slope fabric

C
discard
discard

D
landscape in progress
wrong side of slope

E
landscape in progress
slope

After you have cut some slopes apart and inserted trees, the slope lines may be offset on either side of the inserted tree trunks. That's fine; it's part of the charm of your landscape quilt.

Slope F

1. Pin the free end of tree E out of the way, then add slope F as before.

As this third slope element is added to the landscape, we begin to see the powerful effects of overlapping images. The combination of gradually wider tree trunks and darker slopes begins to create a feeling of perspective.

2. Trim the free end of tree E in a naturally shaped flare with a curved bottom end. Appliqué the free end to slope F.

Foreground Trees G and H

1. Cut the landscape apart where indicated in figure 2–11 and add tree G as before. (See Naturalizing Trunks, page 26).

Fig. 2–11. Cut for inserting tree G

The foreground trees should be of the darkest value because they are closest to the viewer. Tree H, though slimmer, is closer than tree G, and tree H will end at the bottom edge of your quilt. Remember that more detail can be seen when an object is closer to you. Thus, you have the option of choosing a textured fabric or a textured sewing technique for these tree trunks.

2. Follow figure 2–12 to cut and insert tree H.

Fig. 2–12. Cut for inserting tree H

Slope I

Referring to figure 2–13 (page 26), add slope I across slope F and the base of tree G. This is the darkest slope.

Look at the quilt photo on page 18. If you want to incorporate slope I into your border, be sure to use a large enough piece of fabric.

Congratulations

Now that slope I is in place, your basic landscape is essentially complete. Step back and enjoy the illusion you have created!

Fig. 2–13. Add slope I.

While your future efforts may have many other elements, in this practice piece, you have used every technique that you will need to make another, even more lovely, successful landscape.

It may be helpful to carefully steam iron your piece, but please *do not trim it* at this time. You might change your mind about what you want to do with it, or even whether it's actually finished, after you consider the following Wow Factors. Leaving the edges untrimmed at this point will allow for the widest range of options for completing your landscape, as described in the sections on quilting and border (beginning on page 33).

The Wow Factors

In Chapter One, we discussed the crucial elements necessary to lure the viewer into accepting and enjoying your landscape. My goal has never been photo-realism, but I want to avoid an inadvertent divergence from nature that would shatter a lovely illusion.

Naturalizing Trunks

If you like, you can make tree G's trunk flare slightly at the bottom. After you have cut through the landscape to insert tree G, place the cut pieces on your tree G fabric. Fold back a little more of slope F on either side where you think the bottom of the trunk would begin to flare out a little. If you like the effect, simply cut away the fabric on these folds and use this new silhouette as your guide for cutting the tree G fabric.

Several components can fool the eye into accepting illusion as a credible interpretation of reality. Among these, contrast, color, and detail are so pivotal that I call them the "Wow Factors."

Sometimes a technically accurate and acceptable landscape quilt just lacks something. Maybe you think of it as personality or sparkle. The quilt is impressive and you have no concrete criticism of it, but …?

Other times, a landscape will be so enchanting that it draws a crowd. It's certainly not perfect, but it somehow catches the eye and draws the viewer into its fantasy of nature. This landscape is one of those you notice and you whisper, "Wow." It's one that is memorable, one that you wish you had made.

Believe it or not, a knock-your-socks-off landscape is something that you can learn how to make.

Contrast

In every successful landscape, a high contrast in value (a variety of lights and darks) can be the Wow Factor.

Why?

Contrast among landscape features defines distance and draws the eye from point to point around the picture. Contrast in value is crucial to creating the illusion of depth so that we can see ourselves entering the imaginary environment. In fact, without some degree of contrast, we cannot distinguish among components at all.

Not every landscape view, especially some of the most romantic, will have an obvious shadow. Clear light, such as midday sun, may bounce in every direction and cast no long shadows. Diffuse light, such as sunrise on a foggy day, may ease smoothly through the forest, so that daybreak arrives without the drama of shadows. Nevertheless, something about your scene must provide the contrast we need to discriminate among objects. It is up to you to introduce it.

How?

Portraying light and shadow is perhaps the most obvious way to provide contrast in value. Without a bit of shadow, or the suggestion of it, a piece tends to appear flat. With an accurate and consistent shadow effect, your landscape can come to life. Remain acutely aware of the source of light and don't hesitate to include strong shadows (fig. 2–14).

Take reference photos early in the day and late in the evening, when shadows are deep and sharply defined. Look for images in magazines and on calendars that include high contrast, and notice the elements that provide it. Use dark silhouettes of trees and other elements (a windmill, a farm wagon, a fence) against a light sky. Reflections on water provide another opportunity for high contrast.

However it is accomplished, contrast is necessary for a successful composition. Without it, your picture elements will melt together, and all your fine work can be lost in a blur. Test your composition by squinting, looking at it through a value finder (red or green cellophane), or by lowering the room lights. If all your landscape components seem to be close in value, take steps to introduce contrast before you do anything else. Generally, the higher the contrast, the higher the Wow Factor.

Color

Color is another element that can elicit the Wow response.

Why?

Nature chooses her own colors, doesn't she? A rich variety of color is inherent in the natural world, but sometimes we become bogged down when we think

a   b

Fig. 2–14. Strong light creates strong contrast: (a) Sunlight in front of the trees illuminates detail and casts dark shadows behind the trees. (b) Sunlight coming from behind the trees makes the woods seem to glow from within. Both create a sense of depth—just what we want!

only of green, brown, and blue. If you find yourself seeing green, and only green, when you look at trees, you are being visually literal. That's okay, but it will limit your color palette.

To stimulate your imagination, go to the library and take another look at post-impressionist and expressionist work. These artists used dabs and strokes of paint in a variety of colors to generate excitement, imply the vitality of reflected light, and interpret the richness of the world beyond the flat canvas.

Return to the exercise in Seeing Is Believing, page 13, in which you looked around the room to identify how you perceive objects and their locations. Choose something in the room where you now sit, some object of a solid color. Observe again how the shadows help to define the object's shape and how identifying the source of the light helps you to understand the object's location relative to yourself.

Now notice the opposite of shadow, which is the reflection of light. On the solid-colored object you are observing, the reflection may at first appear to be white or close to it. This reflective quality can also be the means for introducing a variety of color into a composition.

Here's an example of the effects of reflected light: Sitting at my desk, I place a red audio cassette box against a sheet of white paper and tilt it until a faint pink blush appears on the paper along the edge of the box. This pink is light reflected off the shiny surface of the red box and onto the paper. As I place a rectangular blue rubber stamp next to the red box and tilt it at the same angle, I can see a faint blue cast on the paper.

While these effects are subtle, they contribute to our perception of the shapes of the objects and their location relative to the sheet of paper. Try this yourself by putting any strongly colored straight-edged object against a sheet of white paper. Notice that you have introduced color to the white paper, and it has become more interesting than plain white.

White light is made up of a whole rainbow of colors. By looking for the reflection of light off of objects and portraying these highlights as light refraction in our landscape, we can introduce color beyond the obvious. This can be a Wow Factor, big time.

How?

How do we introduce color in bits? We are quilters! We love color, texture, and variety. Just because we are making a landscape, do we leave those loves behind? Certainly not! Portraying the natural world in fabric gives us a whole new range of opportunities for using those things we love. We do it with commercial printed fabric and lots of it (fig. 2–15).

We can imitate nature by using unexpected fabrics in our landscapes, in small and varied pieces. We can use fabrics that are largely the main color of an ordinary object, but printed with patterns that introduce bits of other colors. I encourage you to use a variety of prints when you are composing patchwork to represent a sky, water, a building, a tree trunk, or foliage. The human eye will "mix" the colors and perceive a much richer surface from a fabric with bits of color than a flat, solid fabric could ever provide.

Fig. 2–15. Introducing bits of color

Not every landscape quilt must include the colors of the rainbow to succeed. There are stunning pieces with a monochromatic theme or with neutral blacks, whites, and grays. The point is that the colors chosen should harmonize with the subject matter, read as accurately portraying nature (with a little bit of artistic license), and support the requirement of a range in values.

As a final zinger, try using Wow Factor colors in the border of your piece. The natural world goes on to the horizon, but we must end our picture at some point that is manageable. To achieve the mood we want, sometimes it is best to just stop at plain edges. Even then, a Wow Factor binding can make all the difference. If you decide to finish off your landscape with a border of some sort, color will be an important element of that decision as well.

The inspiration to create exciting color in our landscapes is available daily in the world around us. Don't miss an opportunity to drink it in!

Detail

The third Wow Factor, detail, is the component that makes viewers glad they took the time to linger over your fabric landscape. Detail is the clincher, the illusion brought to fruition.

Why?

Seen from a distance, your quilt attracts the eye with a pleasing, accurate composition that says "exciting," "romantic," or perhaps "nostalgic." High contrast gives your landscape depth and focus, and the colors you use introduce richness of texture and imply shape and location of the objects within your picture. Nothing causes the viewer to reject the piece as awkward. To the contrary, people stop to take a closer look.

Now, as intrigued viewers approach your piece, they are charmed by the details that embellish your composition, especially the foreground elements. The hook was set, the quarry drawn in, and the result is satisfying to all. You made good on the promise your landscape extended. Congratulations!

Wow, and WOW again!

Photo 5. LONE OAK (22½" x 19"), by the author. The hot pink sky is the Wow Factor in this monochromatic scene, but it would be meaningless without the high-contrast silhouette.

How?

What kinds of details? Well, scale, as we discussed in Seeing Is Believing, page 13, is important to a level of reality. Detail in the distance can actually be overdone. Therefore, the mid-range, and especially the foreground area of your scene, is where you can add details to support the illusion you are creating.

Texture on a foreground tree trunk is a detail that can be accomplished with patchwork, tucking, ruching, or a nubby fabric. Quilted lines in matching, invisible, or contrasting colors will help support your illusion of water, shadows, or land areas. Perhaps the foreground flowers have a few loose petals, or reflections on the water are enhanced with a little metallic thread. Creative use of quilting, embroidery, piping, fabric markers, beading, and appliqué are all methods for adding detail. High-quality craftsmanship, developed over time by the old-fashioned virtue of practice, is the ultimate in delightful detail.

Your personality, together with your sharpened observation skills and renewed appreciation of how we see,

Photo 6. GARDEN BRIDGE IN SPRING (detail), by the author. Foreground flowers provide details that enhance the illusion of reality. (The whole quilt is shown on the cover and on page 60.

will suggest final-touch embellishments that will make your landscape unique and trigger the Wow response.

The Flip Side

Hitting the Wow response is a joy indeed. None of the steps to achieve it are difficult, either to learn or to use. The main ingredient is developing a sense of awareness of your surroundings and an understanding of how people see.

The same skills of observation will help us to notice when the opposite, negative reaction comes into play. We may notice an error that is perhaps small but so jarring that it shatters the illusion of reality. The good news is that we can learn to recognize errors, even if after the fact, and avoid them in the future.

What a disappointment it is to see a lovely landscape fall short of its potential. It may not reach Wow because of just one aspect, or it may go over the top with so many wonderful details that we are lost in chaos. The best landscapes stun us with a dead-on-accurate illusion. The disappointing ones sometimes have just one fault, but a glaring one.

Look at the fabric pictures in figure 2–16, page 31. The pictures in each pair are nearly identical in structure, but differ in ways we have been talking about. The first of each pair is a balanced composition, technically accurate in scale and perspective—all in all, a perfectly acceptable landscape. The fabrics are common prints, some of them chosen because they are good imitations of nature and meet our expectations for color.

Look at the second version of each and see if you can identify which Wow Factors were used to help tip it over from nice to "striking," the sophisticated term for Wow. In a word, which version has more drama?

Some of us may prefer the first example in one or all of the pairs. That's okay too. Maybe you're happy with making basic landscape quilts. You can do that! The road map is all here. If and when you want to step out, you will see how simple it is to incorporate the Wow factor into your sewing.

a

b

c

Fig. 2–16. Compare the first and second versions of each fabric picture. What makes the difference? Consider the contrast, color, and detail in (a) a stone bridge, (b) trees and grass in the spring, (c) a rowboat in a river.

Wow in Blues

BLUE MORNING is a quilt I made to raise funds for the thirtieth anniversary of the Special Olympics. It serves as an example of several of the points we have discussed about the way in which we see things.

Surely you recall the child's verse that begins, "I never saw a purple cow...." Now look closely at BLUE MORNING, and you will see several things you "never saw." Did you notice that all the trees are blue? In fact, everything is some shade of blue! Did you notice that the land is plaid?

You may notice other things about the piece that you like or don't like. But the Wow Factors in this quilt include the monochromatic color scheme, the value contrast, and the detail. It reads as a realistic landscape although it clearly is not.

Please note that, while BLUE MORNING is indeed very blue, the whole rainbow is represented. Because of the use of shadows on the trees and ground, reflections on the water, and the dark treeline against a light sky, there is ample contrast in value. And while it is graphic and easily read as a shoreline with foreground, middle range, and distant trees, it is rich in detail appropriate to each location relative to the viewer.

I do not pretend to have all the answers, and every project I sew presents me with a whole range of new questions. If I had a chance to work on BLUE MORNING again, I would make the land from a smaller plaid, or dye it a bit darker. I would put smaller chunks of fabric in the border and make the border generally narrower. Yet, BLUE MORNING has done the job for which it was made and raised thousands of dollars for Special Olympics.

This quilt is a winner to me because figuring out how to make it brought me great excitement and deep satisfaction. Also, the results are what I wanted: accurate enough to read "trees, sky, and reflection" from a distance and detailed enough to invite close inspection.

Photo 7. BLUE MORNING, 67" x 56", by the author.

Quilting Your Landscape

Let's get back to that landscape you made following the instructions in Your First Project: Nice and Easy (photo on page 18). There are many ways to finish off and use this fabric landscape other than as a wall-hanging. If your landscape is constructed of cotton fabrics that were prepared as for any other quilting project, you will find that this piece is not at all fragile. It is as durable as any of your quilt tops and can be treated the same. If you decide you would rather not quilt it, this piece could become part of a lovely shower curtain, a garment, or a framed picture.

Of course, you can quilt this landscape as you would any utilitarian quilt top and use it with the addition of other components to make a bed quilt, a quilted pillow, or a Roman shade. The landscape could become a table runner or part of a set of place mats.

Because of its durability, this landscape can be put to good use even if you are not completely satisfied with the results of your first effort. With the techniques that were presented, you can have fun sewing pictures all day long and still have something utilitarian to show for it.

When you do get a fabric landscape that "sings," one that attains the illusion you were working for … when you admit that it really would look wonderful on your wall … then get ready for the next step, quilting your landscape to enhance the texture your picture portrays. A seductive border treatment will make the viewer feel able to step into your composition, as in TWILIGHT ON SPRINGER RIDGE ROAD (photo 8). In addition, there are ways to hang your landscape that will preserve its shape, protect its colors, and make maintenance simple.

Photo 8. TWILIGHT ON SPRINGER RIDGE ROAD, 26" x 22", by the author. A threshold border invites the viewer to step right into the picture.

The Big Picture

Try to think of the finished landscape as a whole unit made up of relevant parts and keep that concept in mind as you work. The quilting, the border possibilities, and the methods of binding and hanging are all intrinsic parts of the design itself. Because the methods used to produce this quilt are interdependent, make your decisions on techniques with one question in mind: What will further the illusion I have established with my patchwork?

Conversely, try to make choices that will not disrupt the mind's tendency to interpret the scene as you have envisioned it. As you add quilting, borders, and edge-finishing, the goal is to enhance, not destroy, the illusion of nature seen through a portal.

Much has been written about quilting already, and I respect your preferences in that regard. It's your choice whether you quilt by hand or by machine, and wonderful quilts can result from any combination of techniques you devise.

Even if you are an experienced quilter, you may want to check out the tips provided here. Why make your own mistakes when you can benefit from mine? Your attention will be brought to the effects various quilting techniques may have on the illusion you have designed into your fabric landscape. Someone once said that it's not a quilt until it's quilted, and I heartily agree. The quilting is a crucial textural element of your composition. It will enhance the impression of sky, water, tree branches, and foliage, and even the perception of shadow, light source, and depth.

Choosing Batting and Backing

If you decide to make your landscape a wallhanging, a quilt that will never be soiled, sat on, or put in a washing machine, you can safely take advantage of the physical characteristics of some non-calico fabrics for the backing. These materials can support the different demands made on a quilted landscape.

One of the things the quilted picture needs to do is hang well on a wall. Your selection of backing fabric and batting material will contribute to that stability. Upholstery fabrics of various kinds make excellent backings for landscape quilts. Even some of my large quilts are stabilized by a backing made of the firm, tightly woven fabrics used to cover furniture or make drapes. These fabrics come in widths that can help avoid the necessity for seams in the backing, and they make a firm foundation for machine-quilted landscapes. Picture-sized pieces of upholstery fabrics, such as samples and odd ends, make stable landscape backings.

Machine quilting, of course, is not impeded by using upholstery fabrics of almost any texture. The stiffer fabrics actually add to the ease of machine quilting because they minimize stretching and puckering as you work. If you choose to hand-quilt your piece, however, the firm weave, and sometimes the thickness of these fabrics, makes them difficult to needle.

For machine quilting, 100 percent cotton batting has a number of advantages. It is thin, which contributes to the effect I usually want for landscapes. It tends to cling to both the backing and the patchwork, minimizing shifting as you quilt. It is inexpensive and versatile. However, hand quilting through cotton batting can be challenging. A cotton-polyester blend will have many of the favorable qualities of cotton, but it is easier to hand quilt. The thin, needle-punched battings are practically trouble-free.

For the ultimate in shift-free quilting, whether by hand or machine, fusible polyester batting is an excellent choice. Fleece that is fusible on only one side can be used as a stabilizer for machine embroidery and appliqué. I have not found any advantage to batting that is fusible on both sides. Experience will guide your own preferences. Whatever you have on hand for batting and backing materials will do just fine for your first experiment in quilting a landscape.

A Balancing Act

The density of quilting used in this or any piece can affect the method you will use to apply borders. For a traditional block quilt that will be quilted fairly consistently over its entire area, we usually sew the borders on before quilting begins. In a landscape quilt, adding borders before quilting can be problematic because of the likelihood of wide variations in the density of the quilting.

For example, heavily quilted reflections in the water portion of a scene cause much more shrinkage than a few quilted lines representing wind in an open sky. These differences in the amount of shrinkage are likely to cause wavy borders and affect the way a quilt hangs.

The simple practice landscape you have made, however, was designed to be successful with a minimum of quilting in all areas. This means that it will make little difference whether you decide at this point to add borders before quilting the piece or afterward.

Quilting the Central Landscape: No Borders Yet

If you want to add your borders after the landscape has been quilted, cut a piece of backing large enough to extend beyond the landscape by several inches in each direction. The extra fabric will allow you to make changes in the borders as you progress. Use masking tape to adhere the backing fabric, wrong side up, to a utility table, one that has a surface that will stand up to scratching from basting pins. Cut a similar-sized piece of the batting you have chosen and smooth it carefully over the taped backing fabric. Then place your fabric landscape over the batting, right side up and roughly in the center. Smooth the landscape gently from the top downward.

Using safety pins, baste through all the layers. Pay special attention to securing the length of each tree and the top of each slope. Pin around all the edges of the landscape.

To minimize damage to the exposed batting during quilting, carefully roll or fold the backing fabric toward the front to cover the batting on each side. Pin the backing in place just outside the edge of your scene (fig. 2–17).

Using whatever method you prefer, quilt along both sides of each tree, being careful to stitch in the back-

ground fabric, not the tree trunks. This outline will enhance the impression that each tree stands in front of the sky and in front of the slopes. If you are quilting by hand, you may want to change thread colors as your stitches proceed from the sky to the land. If you are quilting by machine, you can use clear nylon thread or change thread colors as the hand stitchers do.

Starting in the center and working toward the edges, quilt along the top of each slope. Stay close to the upper side of each seam. This stitching helps the slope appear to be in front of the previous one. Quilt all the way to the edges, securing your stitches at or just past the edge of the landscape.

You may decide to add a few quilting lines in the sky to suggest wind, clouds, or the direction of light. Avoid cartoon-like effects if you are going for a realistic look. Of course, it might be nice to outline some of the elements of the traditional blocks you used to piece the sky. That is your decision, and it can be quite effective. Use a light touch, however. It's no fun

Fig. 2–17. Roll or fold the backing fabric to the front and pin.

to tear out those stitches if it starts to look like the "bed quilt in the sky." You may want to quilt a few contour lines on the slopes or suggestions of shadows from the trees. Just remember that adding significantly more quilting in one area relative to another will cause the shrinkage variations described previously.

When you have quilted the landscape to your satisfaction, inspect the back for loose threads and puckering, and make any necessary adjustments. Remove the remaining basting pins and unroll or unfold the backing and batting from around the edges. Shake the quilt out gently, lay it flat on a table, and let it rest for a while.

When you return to work, assess your landscape up to this point. Smooth it gently with your hands and check to make sure none of the exposed batting has become torn or lumpy. Fix it, if necessary. Does the piece lie flat? If not, assess why. Correct any puckering caused by your quilting technique, by releasing and re-sewing. Sorry, but better now than later! Flip the piece over and, using a pressing cloth and a light touch, thoroughly steam the quilted landscape. This step, called "blocking," will allow the quilt to be as flat and stable as possible for the next step.

Machine Quilting Tips

When it comes to machine quilting, there are a few things I do differently from what others may have told you. As always, I'm happy to share the stuff that works for me, but you must pick and choose what seems best for you.

Begin and end each quilting line in the edge whenever possible, so that it will be covered by the binding. Many times, of course, that is not possible.

I don't reduce the length of the stitches at the beginning and the end. I used to do that, but it shows. Instead, try this method: Leave long thread tails and, after removing the quilt from the machine, pull on the bobbin thread to bring both threads to the back. If the threads are tangled, it is worth your time to use a magnifier to pick out and loosen the threads to avoid fraying and skipped stitches. Then tie a snug square

knot on the back, zap it with a drop of a fray sealant (a needle-nosed bottle works great for this), and bury the knot in the batting as you would for hand quilting. A day's worth of quilting makes an evening's worth of knot tying in front of the TV with your favorite furry friend of any species.

Here are my all-time favorite tips for successful machine quilting. Most of them prevent problems from cropping up, and it's worth making a habit of using them:

• Know your machine.

• Practice.

• Practice.

• Practice!

• Wear scissors or thread clips around your neck. You've never misplaced your neck, have you?

• Hold onto the thread tails as you begin, to prevent knots and over-sews.

• Don't forget to drop the presser foot! Use "needle down" if your machine has this setting.

• Glance at the stitch length every time you start.

• Learn to cut the bobbin thread underneath the quilt without looking. Not too short, please.

• When you need to pause or stop, do so when crossing a patchwork seam. Small variations are less obvious there.

Repairing a Wobble

Okay, the quilt is quilted, but a little wobble in a line of stitching is driving you crazy. Here's how to repair a wobble:

1. Start to re-quilt the stitches about ½" before the wobble, carefully placing the machine needle down into a previous needle hole.

2. Quilt the improved version next to the wobble and then about ½" past it, again ending with the needle in a previous needle hole.

3. As described previously, leave long thread tails at each end of the repair and remove the quilt from the machine.

4. Using tiny embroidery scissors, cut one stitch in the middle of the wobble and also cut the bobbin thread at that point.

5. Now, close the scissors and use the tips to pull out (not cut) the wobbly stitches, one stitch at a time in each direction, back to where they join with the re-quilted stitches.

6. Pull all eight threads to the back and tie them in neat knots. Be sure to match each pair of top and bobbin thread tails so you don't unbalance the tension.

Squaring It Up

For your landscape to hang straight on a wall at eye level, you must accurately mark the outer limits of your fabric scene. Place the quilted landscape on a work table and identify the strongest visual anchor of the composition. For many landscapes, this will be a strong horizon line or the surface of a body of water, and thus horizontal. For our practice piece, the strongest focal point is the vertical nature of the trees. With this in mind, we identify the central vertical seam through the sky. This seam should represent the true vertical of your image, and we hope it is compatible with most of your trees! Using an easily removed marker, such as soap or an air-erasable pen, mark this vertical line (fig. 2–18, line A) with a ruler.

Move the ruler parallel to the line and as far to the left as you can go and still be in the quilted area. Check that the ruler is, indeed, perfectly parallel to the central line, and mark another vertical line (B) to define the left edge of the image. Moving to the right, find the far-right side of your quilted scene and mark another vertical line there (C). Check once more to see that all three vertical lines are parallel.

Measuring 90 degrees (at a right angle) across the three vertical lines, at roughly the center of the landscape, mark a horizontal line (D). Find the upper limit of your piece and the lower limit, and mark those horizontal lines (E and F). The horizontal lines must also be parallel to each other. Do not trim the edges of your landscape.

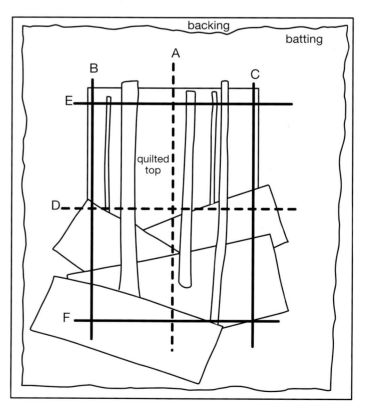

Fig. 2–18. Make your landscape's edges parallel to the vertical and horizontal center lines.

Using a T-square or a large square ruler, check all the corners to make sure that your lines are correct. It matters not a bit what the size of your landscape is as long as it is perfectly square at the corners.

When you are satisfied that these markings are accurate, use long stitches to machine baste around the image, along the outer lines, with contrasting thread (fig. 2–19). The point is to accurately mark this outer frame of your landscape image without using a permanent marker or cutting it at this time.

Fig. 2–19. Baste along the perimeter of the quilt sandwich.

The Bridge to Patchwork Borders

It's time to choose borders. This takes us back to the question posed in the beginning: What view pleases you? You have made a patchwork picture that looks surprisingly like a real view of the woods. How can you complete it in a style that you will love? To answer that question, we will engage in a little self-observation.

The Right Pieces in the Right Places

Let's look again at THROUGH THE TREES (fig. 2–20a) to see how fabric scraps and patchwork components in the borders can make this landscape even more uniquely yours. (The composition is outlined in yellow tape so you can see it easily.) Slope I, the final piece sewn to the foreground, seems to be an inviting entry into the wooded view. Let's pretend we are standing on that very slope, outside the tape, and taking a long view of the light coming through the forest. Doesn't the image begin to look like a doorway you could step through to enter the woods?

By contrast, figure 2–20b, page 39, with all of the fabric tails sliced off in preparation for a standard all-around border or frame, tends to set the landscape off as separate from the viewer. This view is more like a window or a painting on the wall. Now you can see the difference. One edge strongly defines the limits of the landscape view you have made, and the other carries the eye a little beyond itself, thus extending the mood.

Fig. 2–20a. With the landscape edges untrimmed, the foreground slope leads us into the woods.

Fig. 2–20b. With the edges removed, the image is more like a window or a painting on the wall.

Do you like to look at formal, controlled pictures that behave themselves and stay quietly and dependably on the wall? Or do you like to look at images that seem to carry over into the room and affect the mood of the space? To be most satisfied with your quilt, you will need to recognize your personal preferences.

A third option, one I find myself drawn to often, combines these two treatments. By having the inner border define the composition and letting a few colors or shapes "escape" the frame, an appealing balance can be achieved.

In ONCE AND FUTURE HOME (page 9), which is a small picture of my house, the patchwork down the right side adds a fun touch that references the building block similarities between quilting and home construction. Some of the foliage of the trees behind the house escapes into the sky border. Fabrics on the left repeat the colors and textures of the trees and shadows on that side of the composition. Also, the patchwork of pale green along the bottom border forms a threshold inviting the viewer to enter the picture and walk up to the house. Notice that the composition is gently defined by a narrow, yellow green border. It is meant to delineate the edge of the landscape but not place a wall around it.

The Border Crossing–Uniquely Yours

When considering a border, my mind usually strays to my own favorite technique, patchwork. Do you have a supply of pieced-but-never-used Nine-Patch blocks? Or a stack of Drunkard's Path squares that never made it into a quilt? Remember those triangles that you cut the wrong way and never used? I have a shoebox filled with squares arranged from 1" to 3". Do you have a stash of patches or orphan block sections somewhere? If so, your landscape may be their new home. The fun part is that you don't have to make any irreversible decisions while shopping through the patchwork border possibilities. You can audition them all on your planning board, a tabletop, or the floor.

To test whether you would like to make a patchwork border, let's play with fabrics! First, assemble an assortment of scraps, strips, and patchwork sections that repeat the colors and values you used in your landscape composition. Check out your scrap bag for likely suspects. Arrange them around the landscape, repeating the major color areas in your picture. That is, start by placing blues around the sky and earth colors where the slopes meet the edge (fig. 2–21, page 40). Remember to check the reverse side of the fabrics when searching for the effect you want.

Now, sort through your patchwork bits and see if you have something that mirrors the traditional block pattern or shapes you used for the sky. If you used a star pattern, for example, do you have any patchwork scraps of star blocks? To further define that search, look for scrap triangles or any block segments in which triangles were used. If you have no patchwork segments that seem appropriate, make up a few small-scale Nine-Patches, Friendship Stars, Flying Geese, or Crazy-Quilt squares. For this custom patchwork, use the fabrics that are already in the landscape only sparingly, but do draw out a few bits of the colors you find within those prints.

Look for ways to repeat in the border the colors, shapes, and values you used for your landscape com-

Fig. 2–21. Audition scraps and orphan blocks for the patchwork borders.

position. Any scrap fabric or patchwork component is a likely candidate for the border, as long as its presence will enhance your landscape and not overwhelm it. This is adult play! It's a jigsaw puzzle with non-interlocking parts. You get to decide what fits and what doesn't.

After you have made an appealing arrangement of patchwork and scraps around your landscape, go have a cup of tea, take a walk, or have dinner with your spouse. Take some time off and let your mind's eye have a chance to focus on other images.

As you return to the landscape, you will see it from a different point of view. With your mind rested from the whirl of colors, textures, and shapes you assembled, take another look. If you see obvious changes you would like to make, do that now. Throw out sections of the border that seem to work against your landscape illusion, and identify parts that help it to glow. Allow your patchwork borders to evolve all through the process, because you can revisit these decisions again and again until it's time to sew them.

If you like the idea of a slim inner border, audition strips of a bright contrasting fabric or a black or neutral gray. Cut narrow strips of a likely candidate (or use packaged bias tape) and pin the strips on one side or another of your picture between the landscape image and your in-progress border. Again, stand back, lower the lights, or use a reducing glass to assess the effect. Consider using a different color on each side or adding narrow borders at the top and bottom only. Various colors in different locations will produce differing effects, even in this very narrow format. Experiment by moving your favorites around. You are the designer!

So, how is it going? Are you enjoying the process of designing your own border? Have you caught yourself thinking about other components you have not yet auditioned? Or are you uneasy with so many fabrics competing for attention in one quilt?

If the prospect of a patchwork border does not excite you thus far, let's test plain fabrics for one or more sides of your landscape. The visual "noise" will calm down considerably when you lay even one solid or nearly solid fabric along the edge of your piece.

Try this experiment: Choose a single dark fabric that you would consider using as a plain border for your composition. Fold it into a long rectangle and place it along the left-hand edge of your landscape (fig. 2–22, page 41), right over the scraps and patchwork you have assembled. Now lower the lights if possible, step back and assess the ways in which this single change alters the appearance of your landscape.

Where do your eyes travel? What element of the forest do you notice first? How does this single border fabric, in concert with the other three sides, affect your perception of the depth, size, and mood of the piece? Where do you seem to be standing relative to the woods? Do you like the changes that occur?

Now remove the folded border fabric and place it along the bottom edge (fig. 2–23, page 41). Step back, observe, and ask yourself the same questions as before. Try to be honest with yourself, because the person who has to be the happiest with the result is you!

Finally, fold another fabric into a long rectangle. (Use either the same fabric or another solid or nearly solid piece.) Place it along the left-hand side of your composition (fig. 2–24), so that the piece is framed by an L-shaped conventional border and patchwork segments on the other two sides. Step back, observe, and answer the same questions about your visual perceptions of the landscape with this border configuration.

Why do you think I asked you to lay the border sections along the left side and along the bottom? Did you notice that having a strong conventional border on the left seems to strengthen the visual impact of tree G, the largest tree? This border adds a great deal of weight to the left side of the composition and confines the woodsy view more than if the solid border were placed on any other side of the composition.

When a strong solid border is added along the bottom, it seems to form a threshold or doorsill, anchoring the bottom with greater weight but still providing an entry into the view. Imagine what a strong border across the top would do. Would the sky still seem

Fig. 2–22. How does the addition of one dark border affect the view?

Fig. 2–23. How does placing the plain dark border on the bottom affect the view?

Fig. 2–24. How does the L-shaped, plain, dark border alter the appearance of the landscape?

between your landscape image and the patchwork border. If you choose to use a dark color, the effect will be like matting around a framed picture. The decision of whether to use this narrow border at all will direct your next step in construction. If you choose to skip this border, go to the directions for applying and quilting patchwork borders.

If you opt for a narrow inner border, now is the time to apply it. For a defining line ¼" to ½" wide, cut strips of the chosen fabric 1" and the length of each side of your landscape image, plus 3". Adjust the width of your strips if you would like a wider line of definition around the landscape image, but if you want a narrower strip, keep in mind that strips cut narrower than 1" are difficult to handle.

Border Trims

Purchased bias tape, rickrack, or piping could be applied in place of or in addition to a narrow inner border.

Carefully place one of the side strips, right side down, on the left vertical limit of the image. With the raw edge of the side strip just inside the basted line, pin the strip carefully. With bobbin thread to match the backing, any thread you like in the needle, and a walking foot, sew through all layers with a ¼" seam allowance. Repeat with the strip on the right-hand side. Press the sewn strips firmly outward, away from the center, and pin them in place. Now check that these two seams are parallel by measuring the distance between them at several places down the face of the quilt. Add the top and bottom strips in the same manner, sewing across the side strips. Also press these strips outward, and check that they are parallel to each other and all four strips are square at the corners. Leave the ends of all four strips loose.

It is very important to re-check all the measurements at this point. Measure to confirm that the distances from side to side and top to bottom within the defin-

ing border are the same at each corner and that the corners are square. You are making this narrow border to bring attention to it, and if it is inaccurate, that will be sadly obvious. Any necessary corrections are much easier to make now than later. When you are satisfied with the strips, cut the free ends to 1".

Remove the basting stitches and carefully cut away all of the quilt *top* that extends beyond the inner border seam. Do not cut the batting and backing (fig. 2–27). Save any excess fabric from the scene that you planned for an image extension, and sew or appliqué it to the patchwork border sections in the appropriate locations.

Applying Patchwork Borders

The order in which you sew on your patchwork borders is determined by the borders themselves. Look again at ONCE AND FUTURE HOME on page 9. Close observation will show you that the left-hand border (the shortest one) was applied first, the top border next, the Nine-Patch border on the right was third, and the bottom border was applied last.

Fig. 2–27. Trim any landscape fabrics that extend beyond the defining border. Do not trim the batting or backing.

Briefly then, the shortest border section, no matter which side it is, must be sewn on first. A border that will extend the full height (if vertical) or width (if horizontal) of the quilted picture is added last (photo 10). Whichever patchwork border is to be sewn first, trim its inner edge with a rotary cutter and ruler. Now place the border face down on the quilted landscape.

If you did not apply a defining border, carefully align the patchwork border edge with the basted line on the landscape. Match any design lines from the image that extended into your border. Pin thoroughly and sew through all layers, using a bobbin thread matched to your backing.

Photo 10. GUARD TOWER (21" x 27") by the author. A depiction of one of the few remaining towers of its kind (Illinois' oldest maximum-security prison). Can you determine the order in which the borders were sewn to the quilt?

If you did make a defining inner border, align the patchwork border with this edge. Attaching the border with a ¼" seam allowance will produce a defining line ½" wide. For an inner border of ¼" or narrower, move the patchwork border strip (and its sewing line) gradually further inward until you achieve the look you want.

Then carefully press the patchwork border open and smooth it over the batting and backing. Lift the just-attached border and carefully trim away any fabric beneath it, even with the border seam allowance. Then replace the border section, smooth it outward from its seam, and pin-baste it in place on the batting and backing.

Quilting Patchwork Borders

Using the same hand- or machine-quilting techniques you used in quilting the landscape image, quilt the first border section. In general, you will want to quilt from the image outward to the edge of each patchwork border section, securing your stitches carefully and hiding all knots. Appropriate quilting motifs include in-the-ditch or outline quilting and the repetition of organic shapes. Be sure that the amount and distribution of quilting remain in balance all around the border, and that they are also in balance with the quilted landscape. Continue attaching the patchwork borders in this same fashion, quilting each section in turn.

When quilting is complete, repeat the steps for removing loose threads, correcting errors, and blocking the piece by steam pressing it from the back. Let your quilt dry thoroughly on the work table, and let it (and you) rest overnight before applying the binding. You did it! Wow!

Options for Edge Finishes

The finishing technique you employ for your quilt's edges is an important decision. Just as composition, fabric choices, borders, and quilting all contribute to the success of your landscape, the quilt and the effect are not complete without an appropriate edge treatment (photo 11, page 47). As an experienced quilter, you may have a favorite binding technique that has served you well. Excellent! Refining favorite techniques over the years is one of the pleasures of continuing to use a familiar process.

Confessions of a Seat-of-the-Pants Quilter

At the last moment, I decided to let my image extensions pour out, not only over the patchwork border, but also over the narrow inner border. I confess that I was unable to resist the call of a strong inspiration, one that had Wow Factor possibilities. However, I do not recommend this reckless act for a first-time patchwork border project.

Then again ... nothing ventured, nothing gained!

Setting Things Straight

Aha! You thought you had squared your quilt already and were finished with that. Consider, however, that inadvertent variations in the width of your patchwork border, the effects of quilting, and miscellaneous other factors may have caused irregularity in the overall dimensions.

The accuracy of the outer edge may be the single biggest factor in whether the viewer sees the quilt as square and level. Even if an inner edge is wobbly or a horizon line is not quite parallel to the floor, these things are minimized by having an accurately squared-up edge. It's another interesting aspect of how we see things. The good news is that you already know how to do this (see Squaring It Up, page 37).

Block your landscape by steaming it from the back. If there are border areas where little quilting reaches

Photo 11. ILLINOIS STATE CAPITOL CIRCA 1934, 41" x 27", by the author.
A classic double bias binding is the finishing touch for this quilt.

the edge, such as an unquilted image extension, pin and stabilize the edges with a line of machine basting. Use a high-contrast thread to aid in the removal of these stitches later.

With the blocked quilt face-up on a table, redraw the vertical and horizontal lines described in Squaring It Up. This time, the lines will continue across the borders. Notice whether the inner delineating border, if used, or the seams attaching the border sections to the scene, are square with the scene itself.

If these measurements are off more than a tiny bit, some corrective steps are in order. Now you see why blocking the quilt and double-checking the inner border before sewing are recommended. We are not capable of perfection, so we are striving for the best appearance.

Troubleshooting a Slanted Inner Border

The drawings that follow use highly exaggerated off-kilter elements to illustrate the problems we will address. To camouflage such problems, you must first decide which visual cue is stronger, the border joining seams or the landmarks in the image itself. If a highly contrasting inner border has been applied, this element will probably catch the eye more strongly than all others will. Therefore, this component must remain as straight as possible, even if other elements must be altered to make it appear so.

To minimize slanted inner borders, we can re-draw the outer limits of the quilt, using the most accurate sides of the inner border as a guide. See figure 2–28, page 48, for an example. The resulting variation in the outer border's width will probably not be noticeable.

Sometimes, in the course of constructing a quilted landscape, we find that the horizon line has become skewed, or a building tends to lean. Help! This is when Mother Nature comes to our rescue, because there is hardly a view of sky, rolling hills, or trees that cannot exist in nature. I promise you, there are many trees in our own woods that lean precipitously, and for some reason, all in the same direction—poor soil, prevailing winds, "wet feet"—who knows?

The judgment call is yours. This is your quilt, and if you decide at this point that something is amiss in the angles of your landscape, don't despair. You can still tweak it a little visually. Rotate the outer edge in one direction or the other and assess the effect. A reducing glass will help you decide the best balance.

Obviously, there are physical limits to how far the outer edges of the quilt can be adjusted. Go too far and your cutting line will go off the quilted area. Choose a reasonable balance and go on to the next step. Each landscape you quilt will be more accurate than the last (fig. 2–29).

Watch Those Points

If the outer edge of your patchwork border design includes elements that require a ¼" seam allowance to avoid cutting off points, simply re-draw the limits of the quilt ⅜" from those elements, even if the marks are now on the batting in some places. When you sew the binding ⅜" from the raw edge, the seam will be right on the nose for skimming those elements.

Carefully mark the outer limits of your quilt, whether they have been adjusted or not, and machine-baste along this line with contrasting thread. It will be your guide for applying binding. Do *not* cut the edges of the quilt quite yet. Let's consider the binding first.

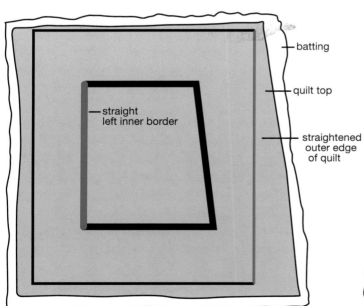

Fig. 2–28. To minimize the slant of the right inner border, use the straight left inner border (blue) as a guide for redrawing the right outer edge of the quilt (red).

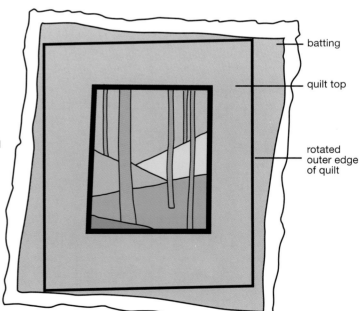

Fig. 2–29. Even if the entire landscape is off-kilter, as in this exaggerated example, you can rotate the outer limits of the quilt until you find an acceptable balance.

Classic Double Bias Binding

The following instructions have been adapted from the demonstrations and classes I have been presenting since 1992. You will find my application method to be a little different, but bear with me. This method was used to bind nearly every one of my quilts that has been juried into a show, purchased by a client, or hung on a gallery wall in the ensuing years.

Doubts about what to do with any quilt edge will evaporate once you learn to make a double bias binding that is snug, straight, and tidy. It looks downright professional, and it's really not that difficult.

Bias binding is very forgiving, wrapping almost lovingly around the edges of your quilt. Because of its springy nature, it is easy to fold the bias in half along its length and have a neat edge to hand-stitch to the back, with no raw edge to tuck under. This doubled binding also makes for longer wear and a consistent finish.

Because it is much easier to apply a firm binding to a stable quilt, we will not trim the edge first. By marking the exact edge with machine basting, you not only provide a guide for applying the binding, but the edge also remains stabilized to prevent distortion during handling. As with the narrow inner border, wobbles are easily corrected. Then, only after the binding has been sewn on, we will check for accuracy and trim the quilt before turning and hand-sewing the folded edge to the quilt back.

Making a Continuous Bias Strip

Binding the edges with a continuous bias strip of fabric is speedy and convenient. The continuous strip is perfect for a solid-colored contrasting binding, for a binding custom-matched to a bed quilt, and for any application in which the same fabric is to be used for the entire quilt edge. It is also ideal for quilts with curved corners or edges.

The following instructions are specific for a double bias binding 2½" wide, to be applied with a ⅜" seam allowance, and yielding an applied binding that is a scant ½" in width.

Fill'er Up!

Perhaps the best-kept secret about classic bindings of any type is that they must be completely filled with batting. This is not only my opinion. It is the standard for quilt judges across the board. A binding will stand up to normal use much better if it is wrapped snugly over the edge of all three layers. An empty binding leaves a sharp fold that can be unsightly and can easily fray over time. In addition, an inconsistent binding may betray a wavy edge made to conceal piecing errors.

If you detect a dip in the batting at the quilt edge when you are ready to bind, there is a remedy: cut a sliver of batting and tuck it into the binding as you turn it to the back. The binding is so snug that the batting repair will not shift.

1. For this project, cut a 25" square, on the straight of grain, from your binding fabric, then cut the square diagonally into two triangles (fig. 2–30).

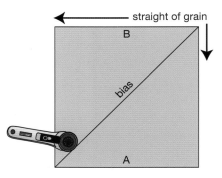

Fig. 2–30. Cut the square in half diagonally.

2. Flip the bottom edge (A) up and match it to the top edge (B). With right sides together and using a ¼" seam allowance, sew the two triangles to form a parallelogram (fig. 2–31). Notice the offset "ears" to accommodate this seam. Press the seam allowances open.

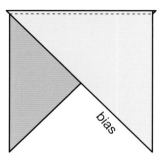

Fig. 2–31. Sew the triangles together as shown, to form a parallelogram.

3. Measuring from a bias edge, mark parallel lines 2½" apart on the right side of the fabric. Mark as many as will fit (fig. 2–32).

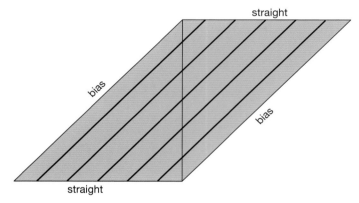

Fig. 2–32. Make a series of lines 2½" apart across the parallelogram.

4. Match the straight-grain edges of the parallelogram, right sides together, to form a tube. Align the marked lines, but offset by one, and sew the straight-grain edges together with a ¼" seam allowance. Press the seam allowances open.

5. Turn the tube right side out. With scissors, start at one offset point and cut along the drawn line (fig. 2–33). Following the line will lead you to cut right through the seam several times as you proceed. Ignore your doubts, and you will produce one con-

tinuous bias strip. The last part of the strip may be less than 2½" wide. If so, it can be discarded.

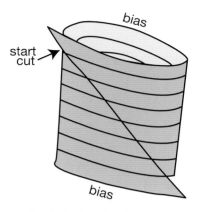

Fig. 2–33. Sew the straight-grain edges together, offset by one line.

What Size Square?

To determine the size of square needed to make continuous bias binding for any quilt, measure the quilt around the basted line to determine the length of binding required. Add 10" for turning the corners and joining the ends. Multiply this number by the width of the strip you want and find the square root.

For example, THROUGH THE TREES is about 24" wide and 31" high, so the perimeter is 110", plus 10" equals 120". Multiplying that amount times the width of the bias strip (120" x 2.5") equals 300". The square root of 300" is 17.32. (You know I have a handy little calculator and did not figure that out in my head, don't you?) Round up to the nearest full inch, so you will need an 18" square of binding fabric. In practice, I rarely start with a square of less than 25", because anything smaller is just too hard to handle.

Applying the Binding

1. Gently fold the bias strip in half along its full length, wrong sides together, and press. Take the time to handle the bias carefully so it won't become distorted, and take care that the raw edges meet accurately.

2. Select a beginning point about halfway along one side of the quilt and place the bias strip with its raw edges on the basted line and its fold toward the center of the quilt. Leave a free tail of bias strip at least 6" to 8" long and begin sewing with a scant ⅜" seam.

3. Use a walking foot, if you have one, and maintain a slow, steady sewing speed, being careful not to pull on the bias strip as you work.

Mitering Binding Corners

1. As you approach the first corner of the quilt, stop with the needle down and mark a dot on the bias binding ⅜" in from the basted line of the next side (fig. 2–34). This will be your exact stopping point, and here you will backstitch securely and remove the quilt from the machine.

Turn a Corner, Change a Color

The fully mitered binding corner is shown made from a continuous strip (next page), but you can also make two different fabrics meet in a miter.

Advance through Step 2 of Mitering Binding Corners. Instead of folding the binding back on itself (Step 3), cut it off 1" beyond the V. Trim the beginning of a new bias strip of another color straight across its fold. Lining the new piece up with the V-marked end and matching raw edges to raw edges and fold to fold, pin it in place. Now, in step 3, you sew the V through all binding layers, which is aso the seam for the new binding color. Continue with Step 4.

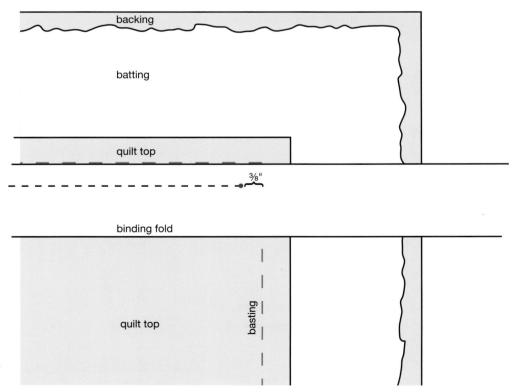

Fig. 2–34. Mark a dot ⅜" from the next basting line.

2. Smooth the strip and mark the binding with a V (90-degree angle) at the corner, as shown in figure 2–35. Be sure to center the V between the seam line and the folded edge of the binding. If the V is crooked, your miter will be crooked also.

3. Now, fold the quilt back out of the way, isolating the binding, as you prepare to make a mitered corner *directly in the binding*. This is not a fold in the binding. It is not a tuck to be hand-sewn later. It is a machine-sewn, three-dimensional turn that will appear the same from the front and the back of the quilt. At the tip of the V, fold the binding back on itself and finger-press a crease at the top of the V. Pin this fold, matching the binding's folded and raw edges to each other. Sew the V through all four layers of binding fabric, but *not* through the quilt!

4. Clip the threads and lay the quilt out flat again. Rotate the binding around the corner and align it with the basting stitches on the next side of the quilt.

5. Place the quilt back under the sewing machine needle. Carefully place the needle down through the first stitch of the V and into the last stitch of the previously sewn binding seam.

6. Backstitch and continue sewing the binding to the quilt (fig. 2–36). Sew all sides and corners in the same manner.

Invisible Joining

1. When approaching the center of the last side of your quilt, stop 8" to 12" before the beginning point. Leave the unsewn binding end free and remove the quilt from the machine.

2. Place the quilt on an ironing surface and arrange the tails of the binding on the front of the quilt, as shown in figure 2–37 on page 53. Press the binding in this position, making a 45-degree crease in both ends.

3. Unfold each binding tail (fig. 2–38 on page 53).

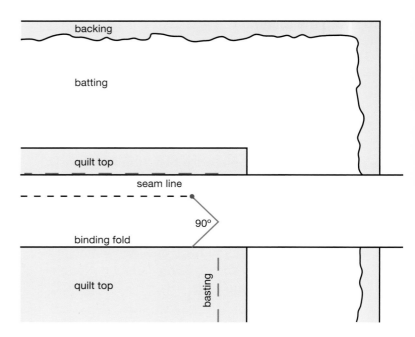

Fig. 2–35. Mark a V, shown in red.

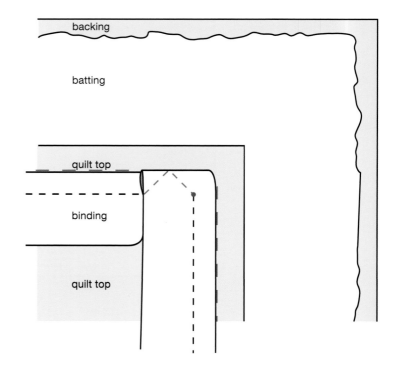

Fig. 2–36. Sewn miter, with stitches continuing down the second side of the quilt.

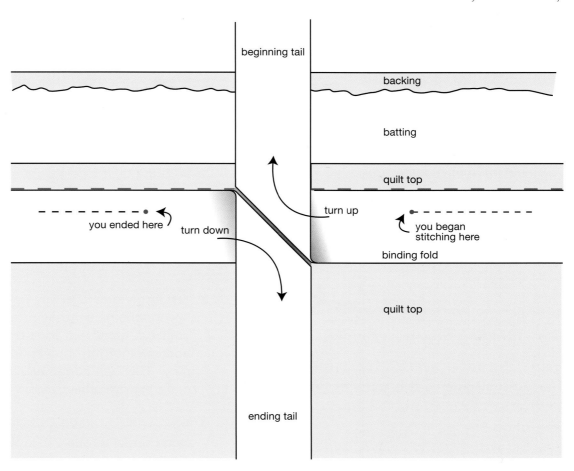

Fig. 2–37. Fold the binding ends at a 45-degree angle; press to crease the folds.

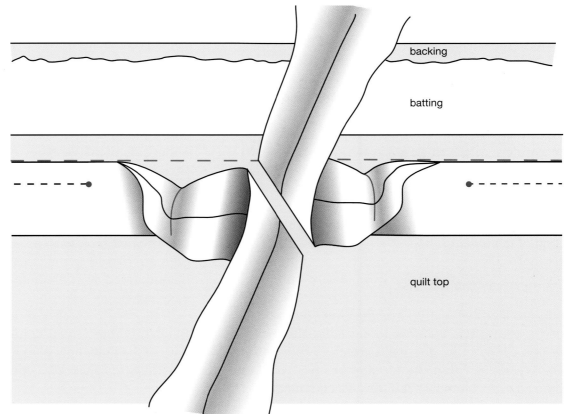

Fig. 2–38. Unfold the creases and the binding and press to extend the crease across the unfolded ends.

Then refold its end to extend the 45-degree crease across the full width of the strip. Press the new creases thoroughly.

4. Fold the unbound portion of the quilt so that the starting and ending points (blue dots) meet. Temporarily fasten with a safety pin so that the weight of the quilt will not interfere as you sew the binding joint. Place the binding ends right sides together, matching the new creases at each raw edge and at the center fold. They will form an X, and this is where you will pin and stitch. Again, handle all pieces carefully to avoid stretching.

Sew Hanging Sleeve in Binding

You can save a step by attaching a hanging sleeve to the back of your quilt in the binding seam. To find out how, see page 56.

5. Trim the joining seam allowances to ¼". Press the seam allowances open, then re-press the binding in half. Lay the joined binding flat on the quilt along the basting line and continue sewing until your binding is completely attached to the quilt.

6. To check that the binding has been sewn on as accurately as possible, place the quilt face down. Lay a long ruler along each line of stitching. If there is any wobble, it is easy to rectify it now. Remove a few of the stitches by cutting the bobbin thread with a seam ripper and re-sewing that portion of the binding.

Cutting Away the Excess

If you are satisfied with the accuracy of your binding application, now is the time to cut away the excess portions of the quilt. You will be cutting through all three layers, ⅜" from the binding seams. This will assure an even, plumply filled, very straight binding.

The following description of cutting the edge of your quilt is the most accurate way I know to do this. Use a new, sharp blade to minimize shredding the fabric and batting. A 45mm or 60mm blade will make a cleaner cut than one of the smaller blades. Use a 24" rotary-cutting ruler with grippers, such as sandpaper dots on the underside, to make an accurate cut.

1. With the quilt facing right side up and the fold of the binding still facing toward the center of the quilt, place the ruler along one edge. Make certain that the binding is out of the way each time you cut, because one of those mitered corners can easily sneak under the ruler.

2. Taking great care to line up the ruler for a ⅜" cut beyond the binding seam, lean onto the ruler with your full hand and forearm and put your upper body weight into preventing the ruler from slipping. This will compress your quilted piece and make the straightest, most accurate cut possible.

3. Now, without shifting your body weight, roll the cutter firmly through all layers. It is all right to use a back-and-forth motion, pushing the cutter through the fiber thicknesses gradually, but do not let up your body weight or shift the ruler until the cut is complete. Whew! You are going to have the straightest binding you've ever seen.

4. Before turning the binding to the back of the quilt for hand stitching, reduce the bulk at each corner by trimming away the tiny ears of folded fabric on either side of the Vs. If you think it will improve the fit, cut away a tiny triangle of the quilt sandwich at the tip of each corner, too.

5. Then turn each corner and push out the V with a blunt-tipped tool, such as a bodkin. When the corners are turned to the back, you will see that you have mitered your binding, back and front, in one easy operation.

6. Blindstitch the folded edge of the binding to the back of the quilt, right along the seam, and it will be practically invisible. Well done!

Shall We Cross Another Bridge?

Patchwork has taken us this far, why not go all the way? When you allow your imagination to take over, the classic double bias binding can easily become a patchwork binding. It will be customized to your unique landscape piece, of course. Another Wow Factor!

Making a patchwork binding is even easier than making a continuous bias strip, and a lot more fun. Line up scraps around the edge of your quilt, placing color families near where they occur in your scene or border.

Assemble the scraps just as you did for the sky section of your landscape and for the patchwork borders that you made. Because only a tiny segment of the fabric will be visible along the binding, lovely calicos, plaids, and novelty prints will blend in beautifully here.

I'm an eccentric when it comes to scraps, I guess. Having once come up just short of the length of binding I needed for a quilt, I now prefer making a little extra binding. Consequently, I've quirreled away scraps of binding from previous projects, already folded, pressed, and wound around cardboard tubes. When it comes time to choose fabrics for a patchwork binding, I can start with a ready-made selection.

For THROUGH THE TREES, I chose from my stash a strawberry print, a blue plaid with rabbits, batik-style pink-and-purple foliage, and a bit of green stripe. To supplement these selections, I went back to the scraps from my landscape image and auditioned left-over slope F fabric and several sky blues.

Arrange and rearrange scraps for the patchwork binding until you like what you see, in the same way you chose patches for the borders. For every fabric you want to use, you need only a small piece measuring 2½" across the bias. Sew the scraps together in a chain, using any angle of joining seam, but maintaining the true bias grain of the fabric throughout the length of the binding.

As you may have done with the patchwork border, you might decide to carry a slope of land right through the binding or imply rays of light by making

the binding seams around the sky point upward. If precise placement of a seam or detail in the binding becomes important to you, do not piece those segments until you are in the process of attaching the binding to the quilt. Waiting to join these pieces will make it easier to estimate distances and make portions of the binding fall where you want them.

Adding Zing to Your Binding

There is a simple way to add a customized bit of color to a simple, classic, double bias binding.

Proceed through step 2 on page 50, in preparing the parallelogram for a continuous bias strip. Before marking parallel lines on the bias, add one or more strips of other fabrics along one straight-grain side, as shown in the figure. When the parallelogram evolves into a continuous bias strip, these other fabrics will appear as recurring shots of color along its length.

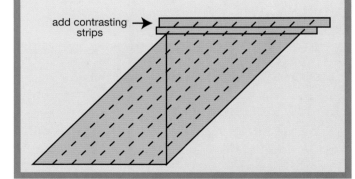

add contrasting strips →

Apply your patchwork binding in the same basic manner as described for the double bias binding with mitered corners, with one extra option. Where different fabrics converge at a corner, using overlapped corners instead of mitered corners is a possibility. The things to consider are your preference, the physical characteristics of the two adjoining fabrics, and the design decisions implied in your fabric choices. Figure 2–39 shows the two bottom corners of THROUGH THE TREES. The mitered corner on the left repeats the angle of the striped fabric of the bottom binding. An overlapped corner on the right marks the end of a design element, the foliage batik.

Displaying Your Quilt

Small quilts, such as the one you have just finished, are light enough in weight that almost any hanging method will suffice. Well-known books describe methods for adding sleeves after a quilt has been bound, but you can simply sew rings or pressure-sensitive hook-and-loop tape segments to the back of the quilt. A series of strips could be used to hang a quilt from a tree branch, a wonderful effect for a landscape. You may like the gripper-type wood hanging devices that hold the top of the quilt between two strips of wood. One friend of mine sews a wooden lath strip into a slim sleeve and nails a sawtooth hanger through the fabric of the sleeve and into the wood.

The Custom Hanging Sleeve

The following method, which I recommend in all cases, prepares your quilt for the widest range of exhibit possibilities. This rod pocket finishes to 4", the standard for quilt exhibits. There is room on each end to hide screws or nails put through a wood or metal strip, giving the tailored look of an invisibly hung quilt. Because it is included in the top binding seam, the sleeve contributes to the overall stability of the piece. It is also an ample size to accommodate a curtain rod or PVC pipe, and its double layer protects the back of the quilt from damage.

1. Measure across your quilt. Cut a piece of fabric that length and 9" wide. Match the backing if you like.

2. Make a double-folded ¼" hem along each end of the fabric strip. The strip should now measure the width of your quilt, less 1" or more.

3. Carefully matching the raw edges, press this strip of fabric in half along its length, wrong sides together. This is the hanging sleeve or rod pocket.

4. Center the sleeve on the back of the quit, raw edges aligned with the top raw edges of the quilt. The top binding must still be flat against the front of the quilt and not yet wrapped around for hand-stitching. There should be ½" or so on either end of the strip, between each sleeve hem and the side edge of the quilt.

Fig. 2–39. Corner treatments used in THROUGH THE TREES: (a) The lower left corner of the binding is mitered, in keeping with the striped fabric. (b) The lower right corner is overlapped, marking the end of the fabric used in the border.

5. Sew again along the top of the quilt at the binding seam, this time sewing through all layers of the quilt, the binding, and the sleeve. Grade the seam allowances so that the extra bulk is reduced. Turn the binding fold to the back of the quilt, and hand-stitch the binding fold to the quilt backing along the seam. Smooth the sleeve flat and hand-sew its bottom edge to the quilt backing

This way of applying the hanging sleeve gives a neat finish and provides a straight, stable rod pocket. It's you own private Wow Factor!

Other Display Options

I really enjoy the "quiltness" of a bound edge for my landscapes, but there are a lot of other ways to display your landscape piece:

Framing is certainly an option for any quilted piece roughly 36" x 24" or smaller. A professional framer can advise you on acid-free materials and ways to mount your quilt. A contrasting mat placed behind the binding will become an extension of your composition.

Making Room at the Top

To accommodate a thicker hanging rod that may cause the quilt to bulge out, you can create some ease. Smooth the finished sleeve downward along the back of the quilt and pin only its ends in place. Then push the bottom crease of the sleeve upward ¼" along its length. Press a new crease in the sleeve ¼" below the previous crease. Pin and hand-stitch the sleeve to the back of the quilt along this second crease. Be careful that your stitches do not go too deeply into the quilt, causing dimples on its surface.

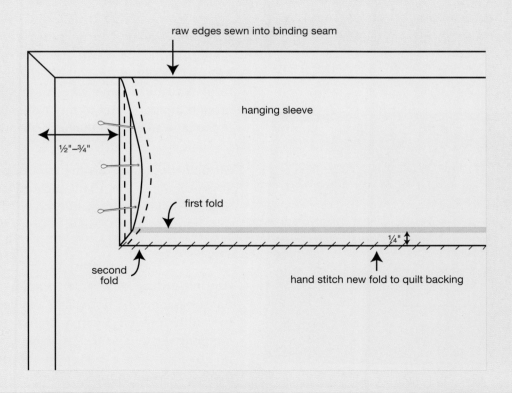

raw edges sewn into binding seam

hanging sleeve

½"–¾"

first fold

¼"

second fold

hand stitch new fold to quilt backing

Or, you may skip a binding and have the framer stretch your piece, so that its edges lie behind a bevel-cut mat or behind the edge of a custom-cut frame of your choice. Of course, spacers must be inserted to keep your quilt from touching any glass or glass-like product used in the framing. Be sure to specify ultraviolet (UV) protection on the glass.

Hanging Large Quilts

Quilts more than five feet across benefit from a custom hanging sleeve that is applied in shorter sections. Leaving space between the sections provides access for wall fasteners in the middle as well as both ends. The hang of larger wall quilts can also be improved by adding a similar, narrower sleeve to the bottom. A length of wood dowel, aluminum bar stock, or screen molding slid into this pocket can prevent any tendency for the bottom to wave.

Photo 12. MORNING IN THE ROUGH, 57" x 67", by the author. This quilt is stretched on a wooden frame.

Wood stretchers used to mount artist's canvas make a frameless way of hanging your piece (for an example, see MORNING IN THE ROUGH, Photo 12). For optimum archival protection, the wood should be sanded and sealed, and cut to size for your quilt.

You must sew fabric extensions to your piece on each side, wide enough to wrap around the stretcher bars and be stapled to the back. Or, a wider border designed for this purpose can continue your patchwork and quilting right around the sides of the bars.

After the fabric has been folded neatly and stapled securely, a backing is often applied to the unit to keep dust out of the back and make a neat appearance. Eye screws, a hanging wire, and wall bumpers complete this display option.

Custom-built wooden frames make a stable and practical way to hang bound quilts of all sizes. Draw a diagram the exact size and shape of your quilt. Build your frame from 1" x 2" wood strips, bracing it with cross members for stability. Sand and seal the frame, and paint it the color of the wall on which it will hang.

Drill holes at the corners big enough for screws appropriate to the wall material where the unit will be hung. Then glue and staple 2" industrial-strength hook-and-loop tape (the hook side) securely all around the perimeter of the frame. Sew the loop side of the tape all around the back of your quilt.

Stretch the quilt onto the frame, pressing the tape strips together. Then pull each corner back, one at a time, to install anchors and screws through the frame and into the wall. This is a great way to deal with oddly shaped quilts.

Any mounting device for displaying small collections, needlework, or delicate textiles can be adapted for quilts as well. Even a bound quilt hung with a hanging sleeve and rod as described previously can be covered with a custom-made box built of plate glass and wood to match your furniture and mounted to the wall to provide all-around protection.

Documenting Your Work

Someone made the impression on me when I was 3 years old that my artwork was worth signing. Yours is, too. A sewn signature on the front of your landscape is a finishing touch that says, "I'm proud of the work I put into this piece, and I will build on what I learned!"

In addition, a written or sewn label placed on the back of your quilt will identify it throughout its life and be a gift to those who own it after your passing. How much they will appreciate knowing your name, the name of your quilt, and when you made it! Other helpful information might include your address, the purpose or inspiration for your quilt, and who will own it, if not yourself. List the fiber content of materials used and identify sewing techniques, if you like.

This label should be attached permanently, in a way that would damage the quilt if the label were removed, to safeguard the quilt's identity and discourage theft. The information can be written directly on the backing if it is light-colored. The most permanent ID method is to fuse a label to the quilt backing before quilting, so that the quilting stitches go right through the label itself.

Don't stop with the label, though. If your state has an official quilt registry, request a registration form and document your quilt for posterity. In your personal papers, include a typewritten description of the piece stapled to a snapshot. Provide a future home for all your quilts through a bequest to someone you know will appreciate them. You could even make a donation to an appropriate institution and provide an endowment for proper care and storage.

Avoid Fading

A quilt displayed for any length of time in natural or artificial light will fade. Even if fading is not apparent, these rays can break down the fibers and shorten the life of your piece. Therefore, steps must be taken to protect it from the destructive effects of ultraviolet rays.

Some newly constructed homes have UV protection on the windows, but even that does not address artificial light. Because your hanging piece will not be handled and cuddled, I suggest you sacrifice a little surface softness and apply a spray-on UV-protectant. I have had excellent results with two applications of a pump spray which dries in 24 hours, providing dirt-repelling qualities as well as protection from light. With this treatment, occasional vacuuming is all that is required to keep my quilts fresh-looking.

Crossing the Bridge

A Change of Scene

The pattern for GARDEN BRIDGE IN SPRING ...

It may seem contradictory to provide a pattern when the goal is to leave patterns behind. However, when you understand how the components of this pattern grew from my affection for one particular element, my garden bridge, you will see how easy it is to develop your own scene from your favorite landscape feature. Let's cross the bridge together.

will lead to your own designs.

Your very own bridge quilt will be a stunning landscape composition. As with anything sewn from the same pattern, no two will be alike, even if you could find and use the same fabrics that I chose. The process has a great deal of built-in flexibility, with obvious opportunities to go off in your own direction.

Making Your Second Project

The pattern for GARDEN BRIDGE IN SPRING is drawn in three sections: above the bridge floor, below the bridge floor, and the bridge itself. Think of these sections as units to be assembled separately, then melded together (photo 13).

Other elements of the design, such as the boulders near the bridge, the gravel path, and flowers along the stream bank, are completely optional. (See full-sized patterns on page 76.) Changes in these features will help to make this garden bridge quilt all yours. You may even decide that it is not a spring scene and choose to substitute your favorite season by adjusting your color choices accordingly.

Please read through the whole process before you begin to make your project. Then assemble an assortment of fabric pieces and scraps in the color

Fabric Requirements	Cotton Prints Recommended	
Landscape element	Colors	Amounts
Sky section A	Pale to light blues for three 6" blocks, three partial 6" blocks	Scraps
Tree line B	One novelty print for the whole tree line, or paper piece the tree line with pale to medium browns, greens, and blues	Novelty as needed, scraps of others
Slopes C, D, E	Pale to medium greens	¼ yd. each, not fat quarters
Bridge	Light, medium, and dark browns	Fat quarter, each value
Stream	Light blues and/or greens	Variety of widths, 12" strips
Stream banks F, G	Light to medium greens	Fat quarter to ⅓ yard
Boulders	Grays to browns	Scraps
Gravel path	Gray print - need not be a novelty	1 strip
Flowers	Isolated flower motifs for *broderie perse* appliqué	As desired
Embellishments	As desired	No limits!

Photo 13 (opposite page). GARDEN BRIDGE IN SPRING. This landscape is made in three sections. (See pull-out section for full-sized pattern.)

families you want to use. Do not cut any fabrics until you need them, and be open to changing them out as you progress.

Templates and Placement Guide

1. Trace the upper and lower sections of the pull-out pattern onto tracing paper, and again onto the dull side of freezer paper.

The tracing paper copies will be used as placement guides, and the freezer-paper copies will be cut apart to make appliqué templates.

The freezer-paper pattern of the lower section needs to represent only slopes F and G and the full length of the stream, all the way beyond where it disappears under the bridge. The other details of the scene are optional.

2. Trace the pattern for the central element, the garden bridge itself, onto a tracing paper pattern, pages 76–77. You will use this as a guide to assemble the bridge unit. I suggest you also use a permanent marker to trace the bridge onto medium-weight

clear vinyl, which will be handy later to align the bridge on its background.

Sky Section A

Use a variety of light blue fabrics to make three 6" (finished size) blocks and three partial 6" blocks.

I used the Rolling Stone block from Battina Havig's *Carrie Hall Blocks* (American Quilter's Society, 1999), but you can use any block you like. The resulting sky will be about 18½" wide and 10½" long, including seam allowances (fig. 3–1). Set aside.

Tree Line B

1. Cut the whole tree line B section from the freezer-paper copy.

2. Use a subtle novelty print for the whole section.

As an alternative, you can paper piece the tree line (as I did) with pale to medium prints in browns, greens, and blues. In some of the "dips" along the top of the section, use sky blue scraps to round the

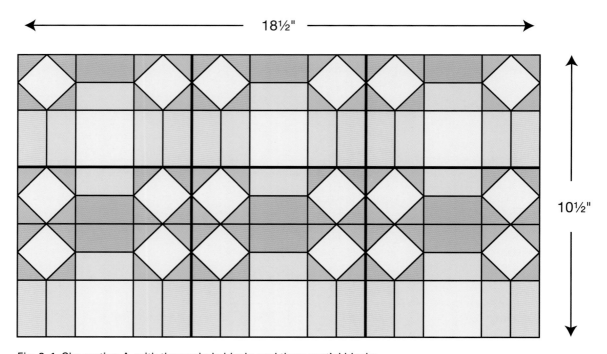

Fig. 3–1. Sky section A, with three whole blocks and three partial blocks.

tree shapes. Use pale to medium greens at the bottom to suggest forest shrubbery (fig. 3–2).

The level of detail should increase toward the right side of the section to suggest that the tree line comes closer to the viewer.

If at any time you don't like the effect, toss out this strip and try something different. The idea is to provide a believable backdrop for the bridge.

3. Trim the allowance along the top edge of the paper-pieced section to ⅜" and trim out bulk where possible. Turn the allowance under and appliqué the tree section to the sky.

You do not need to turn the bottom edge of the tree line because it will be covered by other pieces.

Do not overwork the distant tree line and do not cut away the sky behind the appliqué, in case you decide to change this tree line as your landscape develops.

Slopes C, D, and E

1. Cut slopes C, D, and E from the freezer-paper tracing.

2. Use these templates to cut the slopes from your chosen fabrics. Be sure to add turn-under allowances as you cut the fabric pieces.

3. Appliqué the slopes to tree line B.

The slopes should become progressively darker the closer they are to the viewer. However, slope E should be no darker than a medium value. Use prints that imply subtle texture and shadow.

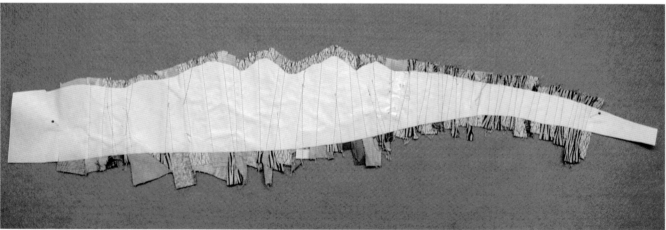

Fig. 3–2. If you like, you can paper piece tree line B, adding bits of sky, foliage, and tree trunks as you go. (a) Front of strip; (b) back of strip.

Freezer-Paper Templates

To use the freezer-paper templates, cut them apart on the lines indicated. Identify the grain of the fabric (or the direction of the print, if it enhances the lay of the slopes and stream banks). Place the freezer-paper pattern, shiny side down, on the right side of the fabric and iron in place. Then cut the fabric pieces, leaving a generous turn-under allowance around each shape.

Turning Allowances

Only the upper edges of tree line B and slopes C, D, and E need to be turned under for appliqué, because the lower edges will be covered by other pieces. To turn an allowance, clip the fabric edge along the curve and press the allowance toward the back. Leave the freezer-paper patterns in place to identify the pieces until you are ready to sew them.

Image Extensions

You may want to leave extra fabric on the outer edge of those pieces that trail off the scene. They offer the option of carrying an image extension into your border, as described on page 43. You can always cut the extra fabric off later if you decide you don't want it.

Remember to make slope E at least 10" from top to bottom to allow flexibility for placing the bridge, path, and other later elements of the scene (fig. 3–3).

Fig. 3–3. Make slope E large enough to allow for flexibility in design.

Build the Bridge

1. Pin the tracing paper copy of the bridge pattern to a planning board, where it can serve as a guide while you assemble the strips to build the bridge.

2. Choose bridge fabrics and audition them against the slopes and sky, both for harmony and for contrast.

3. To form the bridge supports and railings, cut strips longer than needed and 1¼" to 1½" wide.

4. Fold the strips in half lengthwise, wrong sides together, and in half again. Adjust the strip width as needed until the folded pieces are a width appropriate to the bridge segment they represent. Notice that floor beams and roof supports are wider than handrails. Then press the folds, but do not cut the strips to length yet.

Double-folding the strips for the bridge supports provides two straight, smooth edges that will be simple to appliqué. The added bulk also provides subtle shape to the bridge beams.

5. Lay the strips on the tracing-paper guide, paying attention to which ones fit under other pieces and which lie on top.

   Notice that the darker sections of the bridge represent those in deep shadow, which is necessary for the illusion of distance.

6. Audition and cut various browns for the roof, floor, and ramp sections of the bridge.

7. When you are satisfied that all the fabrics provide the necessary illusion of perspective, light, and shadow-pin the bridge pieces to the tracing paper pattern (fig. 3–4).

Fig. 3–4. Pin the pieces of the bridge to the pattern.

Stream and Slopes F and G

1. Cut apart the freezer-paper pattern for the water section and stream banks. Prepare slopes F and G as you did the other slopes, but press the allowances under along the top and where the stream banks meet the water.

2. Trace the pattern for the bridge shadow on slope E, a small but important visual cue.

3. Cut the fabric piece for this shadow and turn under any edges that will not be covered by other pieces.

4. In the same way, make a fabric strip to represent the gravel path going off to the right, if desired.

5. Paper piece the water to its freezer-paper base in this manner: Lay the first water strip right side up across the pattern, and lay the second strip right side down over it. Sew along the bottom of the strips and through the paper, then press the pieces open. Continue on down the pattern, following the horizontal guidelines so that all of the strips will be sewn parallel and your water surface will read accurately. Be sure to leave ample fabric at either side of the pattern for adjusting the slopes.

   Begin at the top of the Z-shaped water pattern with a fabric that represents the bit of light-reflecting water glimpsed under the bridge. Choose different fabric scraps for the water areas in shadow and in sunlight, and for the water that reflects the bridge supports. This area will be important in supporting the illusion of the scene, so refer to the photographs of objects reflected in water (fig. 2–14a, page 27, and fig. 3–5, page 66).

   Notice that the reflections are at least as dark as the reflected objects, but the reflection is usually blurred or fractured because of water movement.

   To mimic this effect, alternate water-shadow and bridge-post colors in each horizontal strip, offsetting the seams just a little from one strip to the next to fracture the reflection (fig. 3–6, page 66).

Shift to clear colors for the water as you work beyond the shadow and reflection areas. Then use gradually wider strips as the water approaches the viewer in the foreground.

Fig. 3–5. Reflections on water are darker than the reflected object, and often fractured.

Water Novelty Prints

Softly colored water novelties may work for the stream. Be careful, however, that none of them says "water" so strongly that your illusion is broken.

6. Continue the water past the end of the freezer paper, if you like, or end it at the dashed line that indicates the bottom edge of the quilt. Set the pieced stream aside.

Optional Boulders

1. Use freezer paper to trace the boulder pattern on page 78.

   The dashed lines indicate sewing lines for sew-and-flip coverage of the boulders, in a manner similar to crazy quilting on a foundation.

2. Paper piece the boulder fabrics to the freezer-paper pattern, sewing the seams in numerical order. Be sure to provide extra fabric for a seam allowance all around the completed boulder unit.

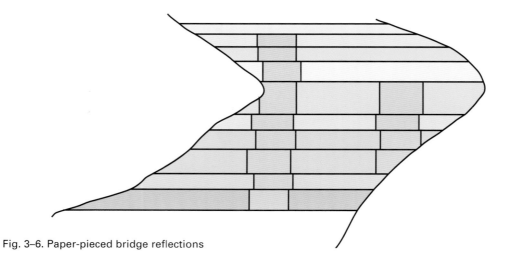

Fig. 3–6. Paper-pieced bridge reflections

Notice the play of light and shadow to help you choose shades of grays to browns.

3. Turn under and appliqué the loose edges along the dotted lines.

4. Trim and press under the allowance all around the boulder unit and baste the allowance in place through the freezer-paper pattern.

5. Choose a scrap of fabric to represent the shadow cast by the boulders and pin it in place beneath and to the right of the boulders. Set the boulder unit aside.

Assemble the Landscape Elements

1. You have now completed all of the components necessary to compose your garden bridge scene. Arrange the landscape pieces on a tabletop, floor, or planning board in this order:

   - Sky section with tree line and distant slopes
   - Bridge unit pinned together
   - Water section
   - Slopes F and G
   - Boulder unit
   - Loose details, such as the gravel path and the shadow on the bank under the bridge
   - Your own add-ons

2. Pin or baste all sections in place, tucking strips and patches under, to look as they would if sewn.

3. Place this mock-up of your garden bridge quilt in a room where you can see it from a distance. Live with it for a few days, changing and re-arranging fabrics, shadows, location of the boulders, etc., as it pleases you.

   Look at the design in daylight, artificial light, and nearly no light, considering how closely the scene resembles reality in perspective, value, and overall visual persuasion. Does each section read as the location and distance it's supposed to represent? Does anything jump out as being inaccurate or awk-

ward? Be willing to replace sections with better choices, right up until sewing time. Then let it go!

4. To place the bridge on the background accurately, position and baste the two uprights supporting the roof first. Then build the bridge on this framework.

5. Use a ruler to check the floor, railings, and roof elements as you work, because these edges should be straight to represent the structure accurately. If there is a perceptible variation from a flat bridge floor and perpendicular uprights, yours will appear to be a tumbledown bridge (fig. 3–7).

6. Pin or tape the top of the vinyl bridge tracing over the background. As you appliqué the bridge, use the vinyl to check the bridge position.

7. Add the water section, slopes F and G, boulders, and other details. Leave all edges under the bridge floor loose until you're ready to tuck in other details.

Fig. 3–7. Place the bridge on the background.

The exact location and shape of each land, shadow, and water piece will not matter. What is important is for you to work with the arrangement until it pleases you.

8. Work your way downward until all parts of your garden bridge landscape have been sewn together (fig. 3–8).

Plant the Flowers

As your fabric picture develops, begin searching your stash and the fabric stores for floral prints to occupy the foreground area (fig. 3–9). Note that the landscape without the *broderie perse* flora presents a clean, restful view perfectly in keeping with a range of lovely options different from the ones I chose. Make the near slope from patchwork, for example. Add silk flowers from the craft store, make three-dimensional folded or ruched flowers, or consider silk ribbon embroidery (fig. 3–10, on page 70).

Fig. 3–8. The basic garden bridge landscape

Fig. 3–9. *Broderie perse*. Not just any floral print will do.

Gardening with *Broderie Perse*

Broderie perse is an old-fashioned technique first used to extend the decorative possibilities of expensive chintzes. By cutting apart and appliquéing the printed motifs onto less expensive fabric, one could economize and still be fashionable.

When choosing a printed fabric for *broderie perse*, there are a number of details to consider: Choose flowers that conform to the scale needed in the location you want to use them. Use those flowers consistent with the season portrayed, unless you are making a fantasy mix. The edges of the motifs will vary from black lines to painterly strokes. Notice that the artistic style of the flowers ranges from romantic to cartoonish to photo-realistic.

Decide whether you will be hand appliquéing a turned edge or fusing the flowers. Hand appliqué is more difficult than fusing because of the delicacy of the flowers. Fusing is the option that will give you the most flexibility in which parts of the foliage to use, their placement, and the realistic look of the finished product. With fusing, it is possible to cut the finest details, allowing the quilt's background to show underneath; foliage and flowers from different prints can easily be combined; and lacy petals, vines, and clumps of flowers can be layered and even intertwined.

At least some of the blooms and foliage need to be isolated so that they can be left intact, but too many repeats of the same blossom may be noticeable.

Keep in mind that the background colors in the fabrics used for *broderie perse* can vary, which can be a problem if the background cannot be cut out or covered. Consider using a permanent pen to block out small areas of unwanted color.

You can also use permanent pen to affect the colors of petals or leaves that may not conform to the light source, or to change a fantasy flower to a more natural color or shape. Embroidery can be added for texture and detail, if desired.

Because the landscape will not be handled roughly or laundered, the raw edges need never be covered or sewn unless you want to do that.

To enhance the three-dimensional appearance of the flowers and foliage, you can outline quilt them with invisible nylon thread or machine embroidery thread.

Fig. 3–10. Sunlight falls across my garden bridge quilt, resting on a design board, as I audition broderie perse flowers in full view of my own backyard garden.

Fig. 3–11. Broderie perse flowers spill over into the border.

Finishing the Quilt

Now that this composition has become entirely your own, finish it with flair. Oversized flowers and rejected prints make great image extensions (fig. 3–11), and don't forget patchwork borders.

How to Make a Pattern

The bridge in my garden quilt is a real one. It is a charming walkway over a dry-bed stream in my backyard (fig. 3–12). It was built in the late 1970s by the original owner of the house, I suppose. It's probably not built properly, and it is totally unnecessary as a functional bridge, but it captivated me as I know it was intended to do.

Fig. 3–12. My real garden bridge

To incorporate the bridge into one of my landscapes, I took several photographs of it from various angles. Then I sketched

a composition that featured a stream, a real one that I found in another place. I knew I wanted to use traditional sewing techniques and to illustrate perspective. This bridge has a vertical rather than a horizontal silhouette, so that went into the mix. It all came together in a pencil sketch (fig. 3–13).

Fig. 3–13. The author's quick pencil sketch

To portray the bridge accurately, I photocopied one of my snapshots and enlarged it to the size I wanted for my composition. Then, using a ruler and a thick permanent marker, I identified the essential lines of the bridge and traced them to make a pattern (fig. 3–14, page 72). There really is a pile of stones next to the bridge—and a gravel path. Rather than lilacs and mock oranges, however, our banks are lined with spiraea, weigela, Kerria (Japanese rose), and burning bush.

Fig. 3–14. Tracing from an enlarged bridge photo

Creating a landscape is not difficult. Just use this satisfying and straightforward process:

Start with your inspiration. Is it a mood, a view, or a specific sentimental feature?

Choose a time of day and a season. Choose the "lay of the land" you love: high desert, flat prairie, rolling farmland, mountain peaks. Romanticize or idealize the setting to set the mood you want.

Pick a source of light and a focal point.

Add highlights and deep shadows, perhaps a foreground element. Trace a photograph of your favorite garden feature … a birdbath? your mailbox?

Keep the composition simple or make it full and rich. Be sure to provide good contrast in value and use appropriate color and accurate detail.

Putting together a landscape is rather like working a jigsaw puzzle made of fabric—your favorite fabric, your favorite techniques. Enjoy!

The Nature of Inspiration

Ideas ... where do they come from? Why do some people seem to get more good ideas than others? How can we recognize a good idea when we have one? How can we carry an inspiration from an idea, maybe just a stray thought, to a concrete expression of that inspiration?

There are techniques for increasing your access to creative ideas, and you can learn them. The first few steps may give you so many new ideas that you need go no further. The inspiration you receive may not be the first time anyone ever thought that particular thought. Your unique reaction to the idea, however, coupled with your unique skills and preferences, can lead you to a quilt that's never been made before.

Sharpen Your Observation

With the skills you developed in Seeing Is Believing (page 13) and the sensory cues described in The Wow Factors (page 26), you can now look at the world around you with new eyes. Anytime you choose, you can switch off the guarded, focused mode that is needed to keep you on track in this complex, modern world. Waiting in line, riding the bus, brushing your teeth ... anytime your full attention is not needed for a task at hand, practice switching on a new mode ... that of observer.

Photo 13. LINCOLN INN, 16" x 20", by the author. A structure of stone and wood inspired this recreation in fabric and thread.

Catch That Idea

Decide to listen more fully to the sounds around you. Take a deep breath, relax, and really absorb your surroundings, noticing the color, light, shape, and texture of objects near you. Carry a small pad or notebook with you and write down words, phrases, stray thoughts, or little sketches. Your heightened sensitivity may evaporate again when you must deal with other things. Don't let a good idea get away!

Seek Peace and Quiet

Nothing is quite so private as our thoughts, and solitude can foster the deep introspection that allows little seeds of inspiration to grow. Everyone has experienced the phenomenon of having a memory flash during the simple, relaxing act of taking a shower. You can decide to plan such opportunities.

Some people enjoy working to the strains of music. I have found, however, that when I am making decisions about colors, fabric, composition, etc., solitude and quiet are best for me. I tend to work to the tempo of music I hear, so I speed up and slow down, hardly realizing it.

Similary, the development of ideas is inhibited by invasive stimulaton. Disconnecting occasionally from the hubbub of other people and artificial noise, may give you positive results in recognizing inspiration.

Grasp the Paradox of Routine

Everyday tasks like driving a car or daily exercise offer chunks of time when we can choose to go into observation mode. Notice the perspective of fences or billboards along the road. Watch the sunlight glint off cars, or how asphalt soaks up the light. Observe the sky and the shapes of clouds. When you allow these to be the things you are thinking about in the midst of daily routine, you may find ideas for quilts popping into your head.

The regular, habitual nature of a routine task can contribute to a serenity of mind that allows us to make new mental connections different from the ones forced on us by a busy schedule.

Capture Your Dreams

Whatever dreams may be, from the working out of daytime angst to random synapses of nerve cells trying to relax, they have always been fertile ground for the imagination. We can use dreams to add to our stock of inspiring images.

If you awaken and remain aware of a particular dream, take some notes on your impressions. Dreams sometimes put us in fantastic surroundings and provide us incredible experiences, seemingly unrelated to reality. Ruminating about our dreams, disconnected from the bonds of reality, allows us to consider implausible juxtapositions of events and objects. Putting familiar things together in new ways is the germ of a quilt inspiration.

Cultivate Ideas

Now you can see that the problem is not in receiving inspiration, because it is there for everyone who chooses to be open to it. Particularly in the act of making artwork based on the landscape around us, inspiration is right outside the door.

The problem, if there is one, is in recognizing inspiration when we see it and accepting that there is nothing mystical or extraordinary about the wonderful senses we have been given. Once we realize that inspiration is available for all of us to tap into whenever we want, we need only learn how to use it. Here are some idea-building techniques that work for me:

Develop Your Inspiration

Learn to recognize it, document it, develop it, extrapolate it. Given eyes to see and ears to hear, you will begin to be more aware of the sensory input you enjoy. Take notes about that input, write your responses to it, use the dictionary and thesaurus to find words to describe it, and relate it to other, more fully developed ideas. When a theme is presented to you rather than experienced yourself, such as a quilter's challenge or an approaching wedding or birth, use these language-based methods to expand your thoughts on the idea.

Move from Dream to Reality

Bring your inspirations into reality by daydreaming about the physical possibilities and attempt to relate your musings to particular colors or shapes. Begin to envision what form a lovely idea could take, then embark on it. Make sketches or look for patterns, fabrics, and techniques to bring the inspiration to life.

Lay out fabrics and tools for various techniques, begin to cut and sew even if your plan is incomplete, and invite the excitement of creation to infuse your thoughts. Use paper and crayons if that helps you remain spontaneous and fluid. Computer users, crank up those drawing and designing programs. Get to the fabric as soon as possible, making off-the-cuff samples and mock-ups of the images that come to mind. Let the ideas evolve, change, and grow as you work. Brainstorm and problem solve as your vision develops. Allow yourself to let go and enjoy the process.

Cross Over Your Own Bridge

Let me leave you with the thought that it is time for you, a capable person, to cross your own bridge. It is time to become comfortable with the fact that you have been given certain gifts, and part of life is to develop and use your gifts. Whatever your comfort level is today, determine to expand it tomorrow and the day after. Gather the courage to cross the bridge into the next novel thought, the next use for a familiar skill, and then the next technique to bring to life a vision you already have in your head. Your brain is capable of original thought, and your hands are capable of learning and honing skills.

Wow! You can do this—you know you can.

"Everything that is done in the world is done by hope."

- Martin Luther

Bridge Pattern
full-sized

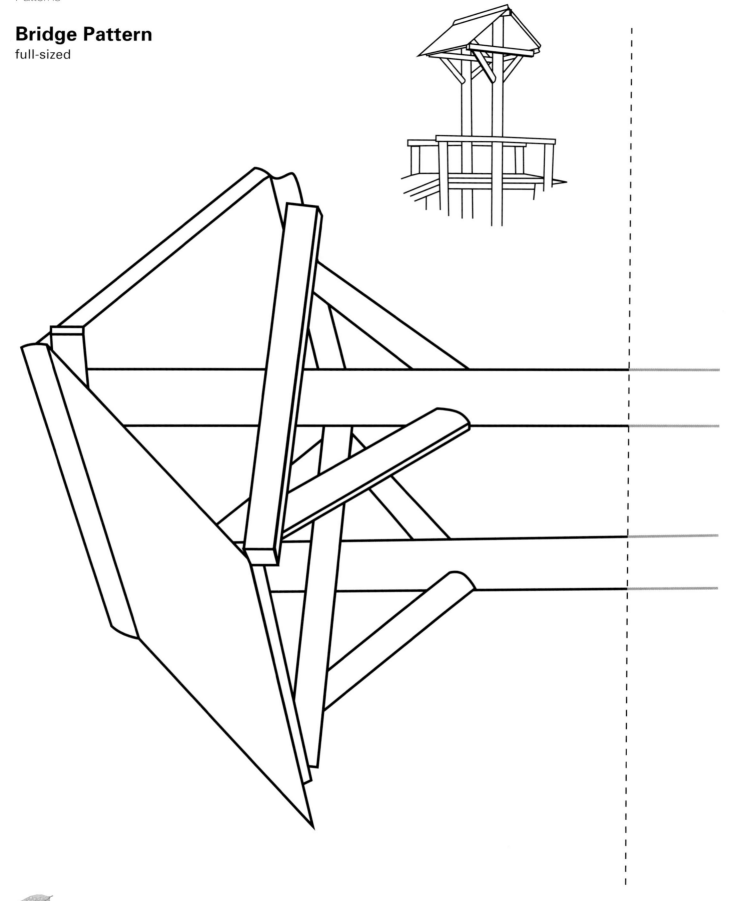

Bridge Pattern
full-sized

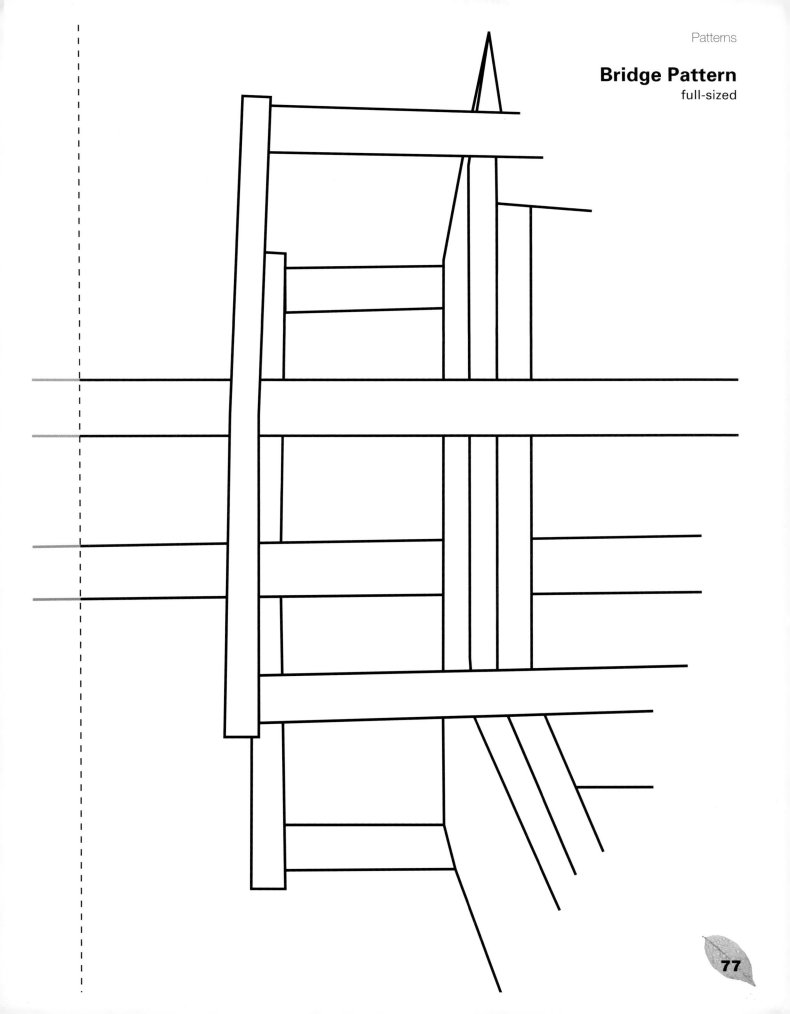

Boulder Pattern
full-sized

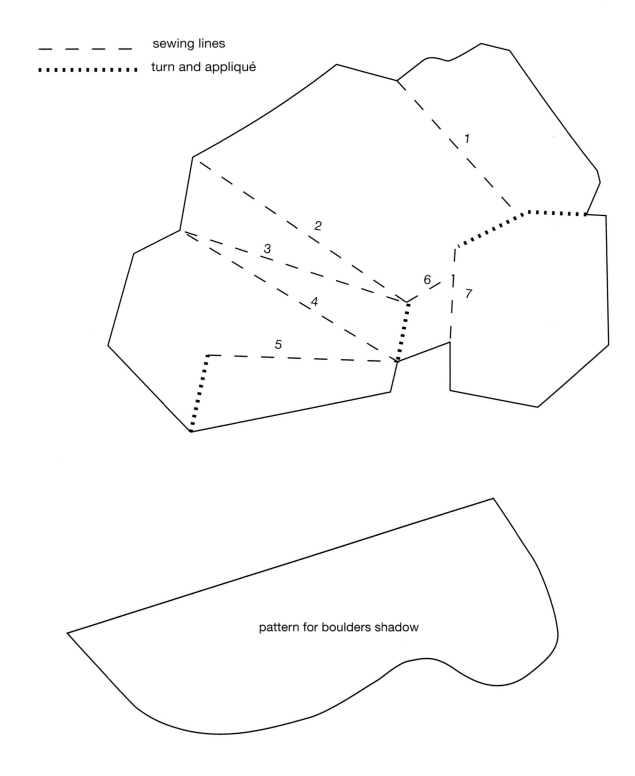

— — — — sewing lines

••••••••••• turn and appliqué

1

2

3

6

7

4

5

pattern for boulders shadow

Meet the Author

In *A Bridge to Landscape Quilts*, Mary shows how she has used patchwork to interpret landscapes she once would have painted in watercolors. Mary's work hangs in private and public collections around the United States and Japan, and she has received recognition locally and nationally. Her quilts have been exhibited in numerous quilt shows and art shows from coast to coast, and she has pieces in the permanent collections of the White House and the Museum of the American Quilter's Society. Mary writes articles on technique, inspiration, and other professional topics, but her favorite creative activity is making quilted landscapes!

While she learned to sew as a young girl and made many of her own clothes through the years, she didn't become really excited about fabric until she learned to quilt. Now every creative urge she has seeks to express itself somehow in patchwork.

You can visit the author at her Web site: www.geocities.com/marigoldesigns.

Other AQS Books

This is only a small selection of the books available from the American Quilter's Society. AQS books are known worldwide for timely topics, clear writing, beautiful color photos, and accurate illustrations and patterns. The following books are available from your local bookseller, quilt shop, or public library.

#6414   us$25.95

#6408   us$22.95

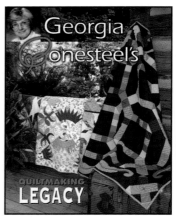

#6415   us$29.95

#6211   us$19.95

#6511   us$22.95

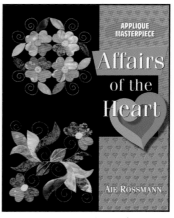

#6517   us$21.95

#6206   us$19.95

#5755   us$21.95

#6204   us$19.95

LOOK for these books nationally. **CALL** 1-800-626-5420
or **VISIT** our Web site at **www.americanquilter.com**